Jonas Brothers

by Carla Mooney

LUCENT BOOKS

A part of Gale, Cengage Learning

GALE
CENGAGE Learning™

Detroit • New York • San Francisco • New Haven, Conn • Waterville, Maine • London

GALE
CENGAGE Learning™

LIBRARY OF CONGRESS CATALOGING-IN-PUBLICATION DATA

Mooney, Carla, 1970–
  Jonas Brothers / by Carla Mooney.
    p. cm. -- (People in the news)
  Includes bibliographical references and index.
  ISBN 978-1-4205-0236-7 (hardcover)
  1. Jonas Brothers--Juvenile literature. 2. Rock musicians--United States--Biography--Juvenile literature. I. Title.
  ML3930.J62M65 2010
  782.42164092'2--dc22
  [B]
                                                          2009028940

Lucent Books
27500 Drake Rd.
Farmington Hills, MI 48331

ISBN-13: 978-1-4205-0236-7
ISBN-10: 1-4205-0236-0

Printed in the United States of America
1 2 3 4 5 6 7 13 12 11 10 09

Printed by Bang Printing, Brainerd, MN, 1st Ptg., 11/2009

Contents

F ame and celebrity are alluring. People are drawn to those who walk in fame's spotlight, whether they are known for great accomplishments or for notorious deeds. The lives of the famous pique public interest and attract attention, perhaps because their experiences seem in some ways so different from, yet in other ways so similar to, our own.

Newspapers, magazines, and television regularly capitalize on this fascination with celebrity by running profiles of famous people. For example, television programs such as *Entertainment Tonight* devote all of their programming to stories about entertainment and entertainers. Magazines such as *People* fill their pages with stories of the private lives of famous people. Even newspapers, newsmagazines, and television news frequently delve into the lives of well-known personalities. Despite the number of articles and programs, few provide more than a superficial glimpse at their subjects.

Lucent's People in the News series offers young readers a deeper look into the lives of today's newsmakers, the influences that have shaped them, and the impact they have had in their fields of endeavor and on other people's lives. The subjects of the series hail from many disciplines and walks of life. They include authors, musicians, athletes, political leaders, entertainers, entrepreneurs, and others who have made a mark on modern life and who, in many cases, will continue to do so for years to come.

These biographies are more than factual chronicles. Each book emphasizes the contributions, accomplishments, or deeds that have brought fame or notoriety to the individual and shows how that person has influenced modern life. Authors portray their subjects in a realistic, unsentimental light. For example, Bill Gates—the cofounder and chief executive officer of the software giant Microsoft—has been instrumental in making personal computers the most vital tool of the modern age. Few dispute his business savvy, his perseverance, or his technical expertise, yet critics say he is ruthless in his dealings with competitors and driven more by his desire to maintain Microsoft's dominance in the computer industry than by an interest in furthering technology.

In these books, young readers will encounter inspiring stories about real people who achieved success despite enormous obstacles. Oprah Winfrey—the most powerful, most watched, and wealthiest woman on television today—spent the first six years of her life in the care of her grandparents while her unwed mother sought work and a better life elsewhere. Her adolescence was colored by promiscuity, pregnancy at age fourteen, rape, and sexual abuse.

Each author documents and supports his or her work with an array of primary and secondary source quotations taken from diaries, letters, speeches, and interviews. All quotes are footnoted to show readers exactly how and where biographers derive their information and provide guidance for further research. The quotations enliven the text by giving readers eyewitness views of the life and accomplishments of each person covered in the People in the News series.

In addition, each book in the series includes photographs, annotated bibliographies, timelines, and comprehensive indexes. For both the casual reader and the student researcher, the People in the News series offers insight into the lives of today's newsmakers—people who shape the way we live, work, and play in the modern age.

The Right Mix

On March 28, 2009, the Jonas Brothers rocked at the Nickelodeon Kids' Choice Awards. Brothers Kevin, Joe, and Nick performed live at the show. For the second year in a row, the famous band of brothers collected one of the top musical awards of the evening—Favorite Musical Group. "Thank you guys so much,"[1] Joe said. Nick added, "It's been amazing. We've enjoyed the ride thoroughly."[2] They were also sprayed with green slime, a traditional prank at the Kids' Choice Awards, a sure sign of their status as one of the hottest teen bands.

Everywhere they go, screaming fans and crowds greet these brothers. The frenzy surrounding the band frequently draws comparisons to the intense Beatlemania that swept the United States in the 1960s. "The Jonas Brothers are an unstoppable force that has exploded onto the music scene,"[3] said Gary Marsh, president of entertainment at Disney Channels Worldwide.

It is hard to imagine that just a few years ago, the brothers were everyday kids growing up in New Jersey. In fact, in early 2007 Kevin, Nick, and Joe were struggling teen musicians who did not even have a record label. Their first album, *It's About Time*, came out in 2006 and flopped in the marketplace. Their record label, Columbia Records, even decided to drop the brothers, thinking it would be difficult to place the band in the current music market.

While Columbia Records could not see the Jonas Brothers' potential, Disney gambled that the brothers might have the right mix to become the next big teen act. A few short weeks after being dropped by Columbia, the band signed a new record deal with Hollywood Records, Disney's music company. The brothers knew Disney had made stars of teens like Hilary Duff, Jesse McCartney, and Miley Cyrus. Now they trusted that the Disney team could do the same for them. What happened next would exceed even their wildest dreams.

Under Disney's guidance, the Jonas Brothers quickly rocketed to stardom in two short years. Today the Jonas Brothers are a global phenomenon. Two albums, *Jonas Brothers* and *A Little Bit Longer*, have flown off the shelves. Hit singles like "S.O.S." and "Burnin' Up" dominate the radio airways. A fourth album was released in the summer of 2009. The band has sold out shows across the country, usually within minutes of tickets going on sale. Everywhere they go, it seems as if fans cannot get enough of the good-looking, stylish young men and their toe-tapping music.

Kevin, Nick, and Joe have also branched out from music into acting. Their first television movie, *Camp Rock*, was a huge hit with the Disney Channel audience. The brothers have also jumped into the world of television sitcoms, starring in their own show called *JONAS* on the Disney Channel. Their first book, released in late 2008, shares intimate details with fans about the brothers, their relationships, and life on the road.

While they enjoy working on different projects, music remains at the heart of the Jonas Brothers. Performing hits in front of huge crowds is part of a day's work. Unlike many bands, which play music handed to them, these brothers write, record, and perform their own catchy pop-rock tunes. The brothers also work hard to make every show great, whether they are performing for a small crowd or an arena filled with thousands of screaming fans.

Through it all, Kevin, Nick, and Joe have remained young men who refuse to sacrifice their moral beliefs for fame and fortune. They might be millionaire superstars, but these brothers still place family and faith first in their lives. As role models, the Jonas Brothers demonstrate how to be true to personal values while still pursuing dreams.

With all their success, the Jonas Brothers take nothing for granted. They recognize how fortunate they are, being able to live their dream of creating music and performing for fans. Helping

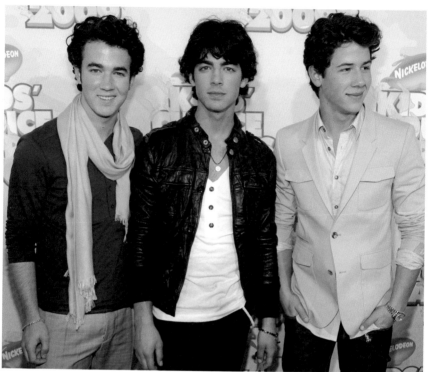

In early 2007 the Jonas Brothers, Kevin, Joe, and Nick (left to right) had their first album flop, and their record label dropped them.

others who have not been so lucky is a lifelong goal for the brothers. They spend countless hours raising money for their own foundation for children, performing at charity events, and speaking to support issues close to their heart, like juvenile diabetes.

The Jonas Brothers are a true inspiration to teens around the world. Their story shows how working hard and staying true to beliefs go hand in hand with achieving dreams.

Chapter 1

Musical Beginnings

Much of what defines the Jonas Brothers can be traced back to their roots. Parents Kevin Sr. and Denise share a strong Christian faith and a passion for music. Originally from Teaneck, New Jersey, Kevin Sr. and Denise met and fell in love as young adults. He was a Christian minister, songwriter, and musician. She was a singer and sign language teacher. Soon after they married, they found a way to combine their faith and love of music. They hit the road and traveled the country. At each stop, they led Christian worship programs for the hearing impaired.

During this time Kevin Sr. and Denise welcomed their first child into the world. Paul Kevin Jonas Jr. was born on November 5, 1987. The family continued to travel and spread their faith at shows around the country. Not long after, the family began to grow. Joseph Adam Jonas was born on August 15, 1989, in sunny Arizona. With two small boys in tow, a life on the road grew harder.

After Joe was born the Jonas family decided to settle down in Texas. Kevin took a job as a worship leader at Christ for the Nations Institute. The institute was a ministry training school. Kevin incorporated music into his new position by teaching theology and the art of creating Christian music. He also worked on his own songwriting and music. During their time in Texas, the Jonas family grew bigger. A third son, Nicholas Jerry Jonas, arrived on September 16, 1992.

The Jonas Brothers' parents, Denise and Kevin Sr., were Christian evangelists traveling the country when their first child, Kevin, was born.

New Jersey Bound

Life in Texas was good, but Kevin Sr. and Denise missed their family in New Jersey. So in 1996 they packed up the boys and moved the family back East. They settled in Wyckoff, New Jersey, a town about 25 miles (40km) away from New York City. They were close enough to take day trips into Manhattan to see museums, Broadway shows, and the city's other cultural offerings. Although they did not know it at the time, the move would prove to be a critical step in the boys' future musical careers.

In New Jersey, Kevin Sr. became the pastor of the Wyckoff Assembly of God Church. He worked hard on the church's outreach and music programs. He continued his work helping other churches with their worship programs. At the same time Kevin Sr. kept writing and performing his own music.

Life in the Jonas house was typical of many families in the suburbs. They lived in a red-brick, split-level house and drove a Toyota Camry. Family nights often included renting a movie and Denise's special sweet potato casserole. Friends remember the Jonas house as being warm and open. Denise was always ready to whip up something to eat for visitors.

The boys attended a nearby school, Eastern Christian School. It was a private Christian day school for preschoolers through grade twelve. When they started at the school, Kevin was in third grade, Joe in second, and Nick just entering kindergarten.

Developing a Love of Music

The brothers believe that this period of their lives is when their love of music blossomed. "We lived in the parsonage house, which is a part of the church," said Kevin. "The church was a wonderful place. It has an awesome stage with a full drum set and platforms. It was full of music all the time, and that's where we all learned about performing and singing."[4] At church the boys watched their father give his weekly sermon and play songs he had written on his guitar.

Every day Kevin Sr. and Denise shared their musical passion with their sons. Music was always played in the house, either on

On Television

Before the Jonas Brothers became household names, Kevin, Joe, and Nick entered millions of American homes through television commercials. The boys appeared in many different ads, including some for Burger King, Lego, Battle-Bots, Chuck E. Cheese, Clorox, and the Disney Channel.

Before the boys became household names, they appeared in many television ads, including this one for the Disney Channel.

CDs or by someone at the piano. Kevin Sr. and Denise taught each of the boys how to play piano. They also encouraged them to sing, holding family sing-alongs and putting the boys in the church choir. Some of the boys' first public performances were singing on weekends for the congregation. Joe remembers this time fondly. "My mom also sang with us and my dad at church," he said. "She has a beautiful voice. Our mom and dad really helped us with our music, and this was the place we celebrated music together."[5]

A Prodigy in the Making

While all the boys had talent, Nick stood out at an early age. "When Nick was 3, I noted he had something special," said Kevin Sr. "This was me as a music instructor looking at a 3-year-old who could do things my college students couldn't do. About this same time, Nick came up to me and kind of looked up like he was trying to see in his head and he said, 'Do you hear that? Do you hear that music? It's always playing in my head.'"[6]

From an early age Nick Jonas was drawn to music and performing onstage.

From that early age, Nick was drawn to music and performing. At two years old he grabbed his grandma's turkey baster, climbed on top of a table, and started singing into his "mike." When his grandma tried to convince him to get down, he told her no. "I need to practice. I'm going to be on Broadway,"[7] he said.

At age six Nick organized a church drama group. He and some friends dressed in costumes and put on skits for the younger children. Church members liked the group so much that they encouraged the kids to make it official and give it a name. The group chose to call themselves the Radicals. While Nick no longer performs with the Radicals, they still exist today and perform several outreach shows a year.

Even at home, Nick performed. "Growing up, I always loved to sing and I used to put on shows in my basement," he said. "Sometimes my brothers would join, but most of the time I was just trying to get people to come downstairs to watch. I would make stages out of tables and all this stuff. It was really cool."[8]

He did not know it at the time, but a chance meeting would soon put Nick and the Jonas family on a life-changing path.

A Haircut Changes It All

One day Denise took Nick with her to a beauty salon. Six-year-old Nick was not content to settle down with a coloring book and crayons. Instead, he amused himself by walking around the salon and singing show tunes for the customers. On that fateful day a woman whose son had been in the Broadway production of *Les Misérables* heard Nick sing. "She said, 'Do you have a manager?'" remembers Kevin Sr. "She said, 'He needs a manager, because my son did this, and he can do this.'"[9] She slipped an agent's business card out of her purse and handed it to Denise.

At first Denise was hesitant about contacting the agent. She and Kevin Sr. were not sure they wanted Nick to pursue a life in entertainment. Nick, however, was positive that this was what he wanted. He pleaded with his parents for several days. Finally, he convinced them to take him to see Shirley Grant, a local talent agent.

Nick auditioned for Grant, and she was immediately impressed with the six-year-old's talent. "He had a magnificent voice," Grant said. "As soon as I heard him sing, we gave him a contract."[10]

Broadway Nick

Now signed by an agent, Nick traveled to auditions for commercials, plays, and more. It was not long before he landed his first major role as Tiny Tim and Young Ebenezer Scrooge in the musical version of *A Christmas Carol*. Although his character was called "tiny," the stage was not. Nick would be making his stage debut for the 1999 holiday season at Madison Square Garden in New York City! As Tiny Tim, Nick had the chance to say one of the show's most memorable lines: "God bless us, every one."[11]

Nick's performance as Tiny Tim opened other doors on Broadway. In 2001 he landed the part of Little Jake in the classic musical *Annie Get Your Gun*. In this show he performed with seasoned entertainers Reba McEntire and Crystal Bernard. The following year Nick landed the part of Chip in Disney's hit musical *Beauty and the Beast*. For several months Nick performed four shows a week and wowed audiences with his singing, acting, and loveable smile. The producers of the show wanted to extend his contract for another six months, but an even bigger opportunity intervened. Nick had won a part in the long-running musical *Les Misérables*.

Taking the part of Gavroche in *Les Misérables* was an easy decision. It was his biggest role to date and also gave him the opportunity to shine in a solo song. By the time Nick was performing in *Les Misérables* in 2003, he was a Broadway veteran at the young age of eleven. "I loved everything about it. It was so exciting to go onstage every day—to sing a song and know 1,500 people are watching."[12]

Through Nick's success onstage, his parents played an active and watchful role over his career. They did not want people to make a big deal about Nick being on Broadway. "I really observed the other parents," said Denise. "I thought, 'I'm a novice, and I don't want to make any mistakes that could be detrimental to us as a family or their careers down the road.' We weighed everything.

In January 2002 Nick (far right), performed the part of Gavroche in the musical Les Misérables *on Broadway.*

Sometimes they'd throw a script at us that was full of language not suitable for a seven-year-old."[13]

Joe Joins In

Nick was not the only Jonas brother bitten by the entertainment bug. "I first got interested in entertainment when I was 10 or 11," said Joe. "Nicholas seemed to be singing almost from the day he

was born. Everywhere he went, he sang. I just wasn't into that. I was into moviemaking. I had our home camera and I would always film around town and make videos with my brother."[14]

Joe was known as the comedian of the family, always making people laugh. He liked comedy so much that one of his favorite shows was *All That*, a live-action comedy show on Nickelodeon. He hoped one day to be a comedian on the show. Even still, music called him. "I was always attached to music and loved listening to different kinds of music, especially rock,"[15] he said.

Although Nick had always planned to perform on Broadway, Joe's first step onstage happened by accident. While Nick auditioned for the lead role in *Oliver!* Joe waited in the lounge and played video games. During the audition the directors asked Nick if he had a brother. They met Joe and decided he looked the part of the Artful Dodger. They asked him to return the next day for a formal audition.

Joe had mixed feelings about the opportunity. "I didn't know what to expect. I went home and learned the song that night and I was like I'm not going to sing!" he said. "I just wanted to make people laugh, and then I sang and I loved singing and it started from there."[16]

Although Nick did not perform in the show, Joe landed the role of the Artful Dodger. Stepping onstage was a life-changing experience for him. He took over the stage, surprising friends who did not realize how talented the joking youngster really was. After *Oliver!* Joe auditioned for the Broadway production of *La Bohème*. After several rounds of callbacks, he landed a role in the children's chorus. "That was pretty amazing. It was a great experience," said Joe. "I think it was really preparing me for what I'm

Joe Jonas's first job was the role of the Artful Dodger in the musical Oliver!

doing today. You know, discipline and all that stuff that's needed for what you're doing in the music industry. I loved the experience. I learned a lot."[17]

Guitar Lessons

Unlike Nick and Joe, Kevin had no desire to perform onstage. He appeared in a few commercials and print ads, but that was all he wanted to do. Still, growing up in such a musical family eventually had to rub off on him.

One memorable week Kevin stayed home from school with strep throat. During his time at home, he grew bored with the kid cartoons and soap operas on television. He stumbled across a book on learning to play the guitar. He picked up one of his father's guitars and sat down to teach himself how to play. "I spent the next three days learning how to play the basic chords,"[18] he said. Looking back, it was a pivotal moment for Kevin. "I learned that I loved it, and that was the day I realized that I was meant to play music,"[19] he said.

Life at Home

During this time life was pretty hectic at the Jonas house. Kevin Sr. and Denise were constantly driving their boys to auditions, rehearsals and commercial shoots. Through it all, friends remember the Jonas brothers as normal boys. Nick was the thinker of the group, intently planning and making things happen. Joe, on the other hand, was known as a jokester who always made people laugh. Friends say Kevin was sensitive and always considerate of other people's feelings.

As the boys' schedules got busier, Denise decided to homeschool all three of them. Homeschooling gave the family more flexibility to go to auditions and shows during the day. "Homeschooling gave us the freedom to be able to get in at late night hours and get the proper rest they needed, do school in a timely manner, and still have everything in balance,"[20] said Denise. Sometimes the family also hired tutors for the boys. According to Denise, Kevin especially enjoyed literature, Shakespeare, and Latin, and

Nick preferred English. Joe, according to his mother, never had a favorite school subject.

Soon another big change was in store for the Jonas family. On September 28, 2000, a fourth son, Franklin Nathaniel Jonas, or Frankie, was born. The older boys loved their new little brother. They quickly nicknamed him "Frank the Tank." Frankie wrapped his brothers around his finger; even today they admit that he is the boss. With dark curls like his brothers, Frankie had a quick grin that helped him get his way a lot of the time.

A Christmas Prayer

In 2002 Nick was asked to record a song for *Broadway's Greatest Gifts: Carols for a Cure, Volume 4*. The annual holiday CD featured Broadway stars singing Christmas carols to benefit Broadway Cares/Equity Fights AIDS, a leading AIDS research fund-raising organization. Nick did not want to sing a traditional carol. Instead, he decided to write his own song for the CD. Together with his father, Nick cowrote a song called "Joy to the World (A Christmas Prayer)." The lyrics spoke of peace and hope for children facing trouble in their lives. The company of *Beauty and the Beast*, Nick's current show at the time, sang background vocals, while Nick sang lead on the song.

Kevin Sr. knew right away that his son had created something special. He decided to submit a demo of Nick singing the song to INO Records, a contemporary Christian music label based in Tennessee. The record label loved Nick's song and sent it to Christian radio stations across the country. The song struck a chord with so many people that Nick was invited to sing at the United Nations in 2004. He performed his song as part of a ceremony to remember the victims of the September 11, 2001, terrorist attacks.

Solo Artist

Seeing the strong radio response to Nick's song, INO Records decided they wanted to hear more from the young singer. They partnered with Columbia Records and offered him a recording

Creating a Stir at School

As early as second grade, Nick's voice was noticed at school. Sometimes it brought a little too much attention. Girls would chase him on the playground, kicking up a cloud of dust as they raced after him. Once the girls caught Nick, they would hold him down until he sang for them. It was not long before Nick grew tired of the attention. He turned to school officials for help. Together they decided to make a new school rule. Nick was no longer allowed to sing in school. Officials announced the "no singing" rule over the loudspeaker system to put an end to Nick's playground problem.

Years before Nick Jonas became a teen sensation, elementary school "fans"—longing to hear him sing—overwhelmed him with attention.

contract. At first company executives did not know what to expect from young Nick. "I entered into the idea of working with a 12-year-old with fear and trepidation," said Jeff Moseley, president of INO Records. "My fears have quickly resolved after realizing just how purposeful he is. . . . He has an amazing sense of acuity when it comes to goals and dreams."[21]

Now Nick had the opportunity to create an entire solo album. He turned to his family for help. His father and brothers pitched in, and together they wrote songs for the album. The first single, "Dear God," was released in September 2004. In a letter to fans to promote the single, Nick wrote, "It is a song that really impacted me and I hope will impact many others. It is a prayer to God from my heart. It talks about all of the things that are going on around the world. . . . My goal for this record is to touch people's lives. . . . So many people are hurting and lost. I just hope that they find hope through this song."[22]

Nick's father felt a special sense of pride in his third son. "I am so proud of my son's first release, 'Dear God.' I truly believe that it will touch listeners with a powerful message from the heart of a child. During the recording we were all in tears as Nicholas sang from his tender heart. I believe it will move you in a similar manner,"[23] he said.

Nick's solo album, the self-titled *Nicholas Jonas*, was scheduled to be released in December 2004. It was an album of mostly spiritual songs. To promote the album Nick performed on CBS's *The Early Show* in November 2004. In a hint of things to come, his brothers joined him on the set, with Kevin playing guitar and Joe singing backup vocals.

Unfortunately, a series of delays pushed the album release back. It ended up being released on a limited basis in 2005. The album was not the commercial success that Nick and his family had hoped it would be. However, it did prove to be a critical step toward Nick and his brothers' musical future.

Chapter 2

Band of Brothers

lthough Nick's Christian solo album did not generate a lot of buzz, his voice drew attention. In 2005 incoming Columbia Records president Steve Greenberg listened to CDs of Columbia artists that he did not know. *Nicholas Jonas* was one of those CDs. When Greenberg heard Nick's voice, he immediately recognized that the young singer was something special. "I didn't like the record he'd made," said Greenberg. "But his voice stuck out, so I met with him."[24]

Putting a Band Together

Soon afterward the brothers wrote a song together, "Please Be Mine." When Greenberg and other studio executives heard it, they decided to sign all three brothers as a group act. "I liked the idea of putting together this little garage-rock band and making a record that nodded to the Ramones and '70s punk,"[25] said Greenberg. Greenberg knew what he was talking about. He was the man who discovered Hanson, another successful band of three teen brothers in the 1990s.

For the boys, working together was easy. "The songwriting did come naturally, it really did," said Kevin. "The first song we ever wrote together was the song that got us signed, so it was either luck, fate or something in between."[26]

Columbia Records president Steve Greenberg (right) met with Nick (left) and talked him into forming a band with his brothers in 2005.

A New Direction

Now a band of brothers, the group faced an important decision. Should they create Christian music like Nick had done in his solo album? Or should they move into secular pop music? The boys knew that teens would be the ones buying their music. Since most teens did not listen to Christian radio, the band decided to move mainstream. Mainstream pop was also a better fit for their new sound. "Nicholas has a more soulful voice, but his brothers are more edgy,"[27] said Kevin Sr.

Finding a Name

Next the group had to choose a name. They kicked around Sons of Jonas and the Jonas Trio, but neither felt right. Studio executives suggested the name Jonas 3, but the brothers did not like it at all. The group's name fell into place by accident, however, when the boys took the stage for one of their first shows. "We got onstage and said, 'Hey! We're the Jonas Brothers,'" said Nick. "That's just who we were, you know? And that was our name from then on, because that's how people knew us."[28]

Getting to Work

Armed with a record deal, it was time for the brothers to get to work. Greenberg handed them a stack of 1970s and 1980s punk rock and rock music CDs and told them to learn the songs.

The boys also wrote songs for the new album. The brothers tapped into their personal experiences for inspiration when writing songs. "A lot of it is about typical teenage love stuff like 'Oh, what am I going to do if I can't see her today?'" said Nick. "It's not stuff that we don't know about."[29]

Kevin described the band's writing process as a triangle. He would start by playing chords over and over. Each brother would take turns suggesting lyrics for the song. "We did demos in the basement for weeks on end," said Kevin. "Recording that first album was an interesting process. We were trying to find out who we were and how to do it. We were so new to the whole music thing."[30] In the end the brothers estimated they wrote almost one hundred songs for the album. Because the album would only hold eleven tracks, most of the songs were rejected by Columbia.

To help the boys, Columbia sent experienced writers, including Adam Schlesinger (Fountains of Wayne), Michael Mangini

Columbia hired experienced writers like musician Desmond Child (pictured) to help the boys write songs for their first album.

(Joss Stone), Desmond Child (Aerosmith, Bon Jovi), Billy Mann (Jessica Simpson, Destiny's Child), and Steve Greenberg (Joss Stone, Hanson). The album's producers were Greenberg and Mangini, who had recently won Grammys for their work on Joss Stone's albums.

The brothers welcomed the help of seasoned professionals. However, they still wanted to be involved in the songwriting process. The brothers wrote or cowrote seven of the eleven songs on the album, something unusual for a new group's debut album.

Hitting the Road

While the brothers worked on songs for their debut album, Columbia Records sent them to perform at promotional events in late 2005. They needed to build a fan base before their album was released. The band toured as an opening act for artists like Jesse McCartney, the Click Five, the Backstreet Boys, and the Veronicas.

Touring as an opening act was not as glamorous as it might sound. "When we first signed to Columbia, we toured, but it was in a van and trailer. We did opening dates, but you don't make a lot of money doing that," said Kevin. "They say if you want to open for Jesse McCartney or the Backstreet Boys, you're not going to make anything. But the exposure level is so high that it's worth it to go on those tours."[31]

The record label also sent the brothers on an antidrug school tour in 2005. They played at schools in New York, Pennsylvania, and New Jersey. Each time they performed, the brothers would wake up at 3 A.M. and load into their van. Kevin Sr. would drive them to the school where they were to perform. Once there, the brothers would set up their own equipment, sometimes with the help of one school employee. It was hard work, but they all learned firsthand about life as a professional roadie on tour. Joe said:

> We were totally for it, because we definitely want to make a difference. . . . We totally wanted to be a good influence.

It would be so funny because we would show up at the school, and it would be like 7 o'clock in the morning. Kids would walk to school like, "Oh, I want to go to bed"— totally super tired, did not want to be in school that day.

And we'd go, like "OK, now here's the band," and we would like totally rock out and the kids would go nuts.[32]

Nick Becomes Sick

While the brothers were keeping crazy hours touring and working on their album, Nick started losing weight. He was also thirsty all the time, but did not think much of it. The family knew he was getting thinner, but thought it was because of stress or a normal teenage growth spurt. His moodiness was chalked up to typical teenage emotions. Then one day Nick took off his shirt to go swimming. Joe noticed immediately how thin he had become. "I freaked," Joe said. "He looked like a skeleton."[33]

Nick's parents immediately took him to a hospital. When doctors tested his blood, the blood sugar level was over 700 (normal is about 70 to 120). They told the family that Nick had type 1 diabetes. Immediately, doctors admitted him to the hospital.

When he heard the doctors' diagnosis, Nick was scared. He did not know much about diabetes. No one in the family had the disease. Just as the brothers were on the verge of reaching their dreams, Nick now wondered if diabetes would prevent him from being in the band. He felt angry and asked himself, why me?

Nick's parents also rode an emotional roller coaster when Nick was diagnosed. They felt guilty about not recognizing the signs of his diabetes earlier. They were also scared that the disease would ruin his hopes and dreams for the future. They worried that he would not be able to tour and perform and do what he loved.

Learning About Diabetes

After the shock of the initial diagnosis, the entire family spent time learning about diabetes. Nick spent three days in the hospital until he was stable enough to go home. He and his family

What Is Diabetes?

When a person eats, the body breaks down food during digestion into smaller parts like glucose, or sugar. In a healthy person the pancreas produces insulin, a hormone that regulates glucose levels. A person with diabetes cannot regulate glucose naturally, and it gets too high or too low. Sometimes the pancreas cannot make insulin (type 1 diabetes). People with type 1 diabetes usually have to give themselves insulin through shots or automatic pumps to keep the glucose at normal levels in their body. Other people either do not make enough insulin or their body cannot use it. This type of diabetes is called type 2. Some people with type 2 diabetes can control it with a healthy diet and exercise. Others need insulin and medication.

People with diabetes have to check their blood sugar levels many times during the day. They also have to watch what they eat and know how different foods affect their blood sugar levels. If they do not control their diabetes, they can have other health problems like heart disease and vision loss. With careful management, however, most people with diabetes can lead a normal life.

researched the disease and how to manage it. Nick learned how to give himself insulin shots several times a day. Because Kevin and Joe would be closest to Nick on tour, they also learned how to administer insulin shots.

After several months Nick finally started feeling like himself again. Today he tests his blood sugar nine or ten times a day. He uses a wireless insulin delivery system with a tiny catheter to stabilize the insulin in his body. The pump is connected to a wireless device in his pocket that he checks to monitor his blood sugar levels.

Nick was determined not to let diabetes hold him back. In fact, he wanted to turn his experience into an opportunity to help other kids with the disease. "At first I was worried that diabetes would keep me from performing and recording and doing everything a teenager likes to do," he said. "I want to let kids know that it doesn't have to be so hard. The most important thing is to never, ever let yourself get down about having diabetes, because you can live a really great life as a kid with diabetes."[34]

First Single Released

In December 2005 the Jonas Brothers released their first single, "Mandy." A childhood friend inspired the song. "I was actually dating Joseph when the song came out," Mandy said. "I was in their kitchen and they sat me down and said we have something to tell you. They played the song, and I didn't believe it."[35]

While Mandy and Joe's romance did not last, their friendship did. The single became the Jonas Brothers' first hit. In March 2006 the "Mandy" video premiered on MTV's *Total Request Live*. With their first single and video doing well, the band's popularity was on the rise. Now the brothers looked forward to the release of their album.

Practicing Onstage

Not long after the school tours ended, Columbia announced the Jonas Brothers would hit the road again for their American Club Tour. The record label scheduled the band's upcoming album for release on April 11, 2006. Label executives designed the tour to promote the debut album. The Jonas Brothers played in smaller, intimate club settings across the country from late January through March 2006.

Despite a grueling schedule, every performance gave the brothers a chance to practice their stage presence and interact with the crowd. During this time, they developed their own personalities onstage. Kevin explained:

> I'm pretty much stationary, just singing and playing my guitar. . . . But Joseph and Nick, they run and do a ton. They jump around all over the place. Sometimes, if someone in the front row isn't paying attention, Joseph will run over and tap her on the shoulder and just start singing in her face. The time he did that the girl just started freaking out and loving it. It's a way to get everyone involved.[36]

Nick credits his Broadway training with helping him connect with the crowds onstage. However, he thinks that performing as a band is different than being part of a show. With the band there are only three people onstage. There is a lot more pressure on each person to set the mood of the show. Each one has to work to make the show great. If one person is having a down day, there are only two others to pick up the slack.

Kevin, Joe, and Nick appear on MTV's Total Request Live in March 2006 to promote their song "Mandy."

The performances also showed off each brother's talents. According to Joe, Nick's young, soulful voice was the group's powerhouse vocal. And Nick says: "Joseph just has this really cool, smooth rock voice. . . . He really knows how to get the crowd going. Kevin is the one that holds us all together. Joe and I are the singers and we take turns on keyboards, and percussion, but Kevin mostly plays the guitar and that's the part of the group that we need—he's the glue that keeps it together."[37]

Loving the Daily Grind

Constant touring and recording was hard work. "Most people don't understand how much work it really takes," Nick said. "You have to keep doing it, every day, trying . . . [to] build up your voice throughout the entire day, and then you have a show at like 10 o'clock at night."[38] Still, the brothers enjoyed every minute. "It gets tiring, but you know, the fact of when you get back on that stage, it's worth every bit," Joe said. "Every bit of energy that you spend to get there, it's completely worth it."[39]

The Jonas Brothers worked hard on their grueling tour schedule. Performing as opening acts in schools and in venues around the country started a grassroots buzz about their music. After every show they would check their MySpace page. Each time there were more friend requests. Everything seemed to be falling

Five Fast Facts— Kevin Jonas

- Kevin's favorite kind of ice cream is rocky road.
- His favorite sport is golf.
- Kevin collects Gibson Les Paul guitars.
- If he were not a pop star, Kevin would like to be an astronaut.
- He cannot live without his cell phone and BlackBerry wireless device.

into place. Their first single and video were doing well, and their fan base was growing. Now the boys waited in excitement for the release of their debut album. Unfortunately, it would take much longer than expected.

In July 2006, while waiting for Columbia to release their CD, It's About Time, *the boys hosted various events for Radio Disney, including the Totally Ten Birthday Concert in Anaheim, California.*

More Delays

The Jonas Brothers' debut album was originally scheduled to appear in April 2006. Studio executives, however, kept pushing back the release date. The band's manager, Phil McIntyre, estimated that they probably had about ten different release dates. Although the brothers felt good about their original version, the record label kept sending them back to the recording studio. Executives wanted a few more tracks and another lead single.

The band found another single in "Year 3000." It was a song originally done by the English pop-punk band Busted. It had been a 2002 hit in the United Kingdom. The song, however, had not translated its UK success to the United States. In 2006 the Jonas Brothers recorded their own version of the song and added it to their album.

The brothers also did some more promo work while they waited for their album to be released. One of the songs from their album, "Time for Me to Fly," appeared on the *Aquamarine* movie soundtrack. Their single "Mandy" aired on Nickelodeon's television movie *Zoey 101: Spring Break-Up*. They recorded a cover of "Yo Ho (A Pirate's Life for Me)" for the April 2006 *DisneyMania 4* CD. They also sang the new theme song for the Disney Channel show *American Dragon: Jake Long* that debuted in the summer of 2006.

The brothers had spent long hours working on their album. They spent even more time touring and promoting the debut. Despite all their effort Columbia continued to hold the album's release. By the summer of 2006, there was still no album.

It's About Time

On August 8, 2006, the waiting finally ended. After what seemed like endless delays, Columbia finally released the band's first album, *It's About Time*. It had been a long wait, but the brothers were excited. Nick said:

> Even though we're young, we've been waiting for this a long time. It feels like it's been forever. The name of the album is really true, but there's a cool double meaning to it. We've got the fact that [the album] is finally out, so it's

about time it came out. But also a lot of the songs on the record are about time—like "One Day at a Time," "Time for Me to Fly" and "Year 3000."[40]

The brothers were proud of the album they had made. They felt like all the hard work and long hours were finally worth it. When *It's About Time* entered the Billboard 200 at number ninety-one, the band members could hardly contain their excitement. Unfortunately, this album would not live up to their high expectations.

Missing the Mark

The record hit stores in a limited release with about fifty thousand copies on the market. It was barely noticed. After spending so much time writing, recording, and touring, the brothers were extremely disappointed by the album's lackluster reception.

Some of the blame for the album's weak sales fell at Columbia's feet. According to the band's manager, Phil McIntyre, Columbia did not appear to have a plan in place for the band. "That was disappointing," McIntyre said. "We'd never gone to top 40, and Sony [Columbia] never put together a proper radio plan. Steve Greenberg did an amazing job of imagining a fan base at a grass-roots level, but we were missing that key exposure."[41]

Even worse, management changes at Columbia left the Jonas Brothers drifting without direction. Their chief supporter, Greenberg, had recently left the record label. Without Greenberg behind them, the brothers felt as if the label did not know where to position them in the market.

Small Successes

Meanwhile, the end of 2006 brought a few small successes for the band. Nick's "Joy to the World" solo single appeared on *Joy to the World: The Ultimate Christmas Collection* in October. "Year 3000" gained airplay on Radio Disney. And the brothers also recorded another cover for Disney. This time they sang "Poor Unfortunate Souls" for *The Little Mermaid* movie soundtrack.

The Bonus Jonas

Born on September 28, 2000, Franklin Nathaniel Jonas, also known as Frankie, is the fourth Jonas brother. A late addition to the family, Frankie is called the "Bonus Jonas" by fans. Despite having world-famous brothers, Frankie is a lot like other kids his age. He likes to play video games and watch the Disney Channel cartoon *Phineas and Ferb*.

Frankie has gotten onstage a few times with his brothers, much to fans' delight. He too has been bitten by the music bug and plays drums. But Frankie insists that he is not joining his brothers' band. Instead, he plans to strike out on his own. In fact, he and a friend have already formed their own band.

Fans have come to know the Bonus Jonas so well that they scream his name at events. They will be getting to see a lot more of him in the future. Frankie joined his brothers in their

new Disney Channel show, *JONAS*, which premiered in May 2009. He is also on tap to act with his brothers in a big-screen adaptation of the popular children's book *Walter the Farting Dog*.

The youngest Jonas brother, Frankie, known as the "Bonus Jonas," has decided to form his own band.

Too Little, Too Late

By the fall of 2006, the Jonas Brothers were unhappy with Columbia's handling of their album. They felt the label was not giving them the support they deserved. Even more concerning, they did not see the label's plan for their future. So the brothers decided to meet with label executives. They were thinking about leaving Columbia, but they wanted to talk to the executives before they made any decisions. At the meeting record label executives told the brothers that the label was not ready to move forward with their next album. "The reason given to us was 'The indicators were not there,'" said Kevin Sr. "It was devastating."[42]

The brothers thought they would end 2006 celebrating their first album together and starting work on a second. Instead, they found themselves without a record label. It was one of the lowest points of their career. Unknown to the band, however, a new opportunity was just around the corner.

Chapter 3

Joining the Disney Family

The Jonas Brothers entered 2007 with uncertainty. They did not have a record label or a clear direction for the future. Their debut album had struggled. Some people might have given up on their dreams after being dealt similar disappointments. The Jonas Brothers did not. They believed in themselves and their talent. Within a few short weeks, their faith would prove to be right.

Disney Steps In

In 2006 the brothers had recorded a song for a *DisneyMania* CD and performed as the opening act for Disney artist Jesse McCartney. While they worked on Disney projects, the Jonas Brothers' fresh, clean style and catchy songs caught Disney executives' attention.

In the early years of the twenty-first century, the Disney channel had developed into a powerhouse cable channel by featuring original shows for teens and tweens. Kids loved hit shows like *Lizzie McGuire*, *That's So Raven*, and *The Suite Life of Zack & Cody*. In 2006 the Disney Channel's popularity exploded even more with *High School Musical* and *Hannah Montana*.

Disney had a proven track record of successfully discovering and promoting teen stars who could also sing. Their record label, Hollywood Records, opened in 1989. It launched the musical careers of Disney talent like the Cheetah Girls, Jesse McCartney, Hilary Duff, Vanessa Hudgens, and Miley Cyrus.

In 2006 the Jonas Brothers were the opening act for Disney artist Jesse McCartney (pictured) and were also involved in other Disney projects.

In early 2007 Disney and Hollywood Records were searching for the next breakout act. "We've been incredibly successful in the teen-pop field," said Abbey Konowitch, Hollywood Records' general manager. "But we've been looking for a boy band. And here was one that was already developed."[43]

The Jonas Brothers fit every criterion that Hollywood Records and Disney looked for in new talent. They had a great pop sound. Kids could relate to their music. The good-looking, stylish brothers made the girls go crazy. Also, their squeaky-clean background and image fit perfectly with the Disney brand. While Columbia Records had struggled to position the band, Disney immediately recognized its tremendous potential. Within a few weeks they offered the brothers a contract.

New Record Deal

The Jonas Brothers signed their record deal with Hollywood Records on February 8, 2007. Only a few weeks after leaving Columbia, the band was thrilled to have found a new record label so quickly. In a statement they said: "We are fortunate to have this incredible opportunity to deliver noteworthy music to our fans. To continue building our careers in this industry with Hollywood Records is one step closer in achieving our dreams."[44]

Steve Greenberg, the former Columbia executive who had originally signed the band, wished the brothers luck at their new label. "Hopefully Disney takes them down the same road I did," he said. "The guys are so good at what they do that it's going to work if they're allowed to pursue their own vision. The smartest thing a label can do is not mess with them."[45]

Baby Bottle Pops

The brothers received more good news in February 2007. They inked their first endorsement deal with Topps Confections, a leading kids' candy company. The Jonas Brothers would promote the company's popular Baby Bottle Pops. Ari Weinstock, Topps brand manager, said:

We are thrilled to partner with the Jonas Brothers and have them be the centerpiece of our Baby Bottle Pop integrated marketing plan, which includes online, mobile, television, print, a sweepstakes and concert tour. The Jonas Brothers' re-imagining of the Baby Bottle Pop theme song will have kids rockin' out to one of the favorite theme songs sung by one of today's hottest new groups.[46]

The Jonas boys appear at an elementary school as part of Topps Confections' promotion for the popular Baby Bottle Pops in May 2008.

No Time to Waste

As soon as the brothers signed, Hollywood Records sent them to work on their next album. On their first album the brothers had worked with professional songwriters. At times they had felt like they had lost control of the album's direction. This time they wanted to make sure they were involved in every step of the process.

The brothers teamed up with producer John Fields. Fields had worked with successful artists such as Lifehouse, Switchfoot, and Rooney. The boys admired his past work and were excited to have the chance to work with him on their second album.

As soon as the brothers met Fields, they felt a connection. They liked how he was open to their ideas and input. Kevin explained:

> The album was very much a collaborative process. It's definitely our baby, but John completely understood our vision and made sure we were there to help him guide the process every day of the recording process. We rented out a house in Studio City that we called "Rock House," living there for the whole month of February (2007) and working from 11 A.M. to 11 P.M. in the attached facility called Underbelly Studios. It was a really awesome, one of a kind experience.[47]

Fields worked fast. It had taken the brothers almost a year and a half to complete the recording of their first album. This time they finished in twenty-one days. The new album would have twelve new tracks. Two previously recorded songs, "Year 3000" and "Kids of the Future," were also included as bonus tracks.

The brothers' experiences over the past two years helped them as they recorded the new album. Nick elaborated:

> When we did *It's About Time* it was the first record we had ever done, and we have so much more experience to draw from now, both from doing so many live shows to spending all that time in the studio. We've had two more years now to become more proficient on our instruments and do all the things we needed to become a better band. We were a much bigger part of everything that happened this time.[48]

For their second CD the boys not only wrote the songs but also played their own instruments.

Getting Personal

Just as they wanted, the boys were more involved with their second album. They wrote or cowrote all twelve new tracks. According to Nick, the lyrics on their second album were filled with more personal experiences. The ups and downs over the past few years had given them material to write about and helped them to evolve as songwriters and musicians. He hoped that writing about topics close to their hearts would help the band connect even more with fans.

The brothers did more than just write and sing the songs on their album. Unlike some singing groups, the Jonas Brothers also played their own instruments. Kevin played lead guitar. Joe played guitar and keyboards. Nick contributed on guitar, keyboards, and drums. It really was an all-Jonas effort.

The brothers were proud of their new album. They felt like the lyrics and music were more advanced. The entire album felt tighter than their first. Because they had put so much of themselves into the making of this album, they decided to use their name for the album title, *Jonas Brothers*.

The Disney Marketing Machine

As soon as the band signed with Hollywood Records, the Disney marketing machine kicked into gear. "Kevin, Joe and Nick are the real deal—incredible musicians, phenomenal performers, charismatic stars. An act like the Jonas Brothers doesn't come along very often. This is a giant coup for the Disney Channel,"[49] said Gary Marsh, president of entertainment for Disney Channel Worldwide.

Almost immediately, Disney launched a plan to cross-promote the band on radio, television, music, and film. Radio Disney played music from the band's first album while waiting for the second. The Disney Channel aired Jonas Brothers music videos often, sometimes as many as fifty times per week. Disney also had the band record more songs for other projects. In April 2007 the Jonas Brothers recorded "I Wanna Be Like You" for the *DisneyMania 5* album. Their single "Kids of the Future" landed on the *Meet the Robinsons* movie soundtrack. Disney also sent the band on promotional mall concerts around the country.

The Jonas Brothers quickly noticed the difference in exposure with Disney behind them. After their videos aired on the Disney Channel, more people came to their concerts. Their MySpace page exploded with friend requests. After one month with Disney, the band gathered more fans than it had during the past two years.

The Marvelous Party Tour

The brothers kicked off the Marvelous Party Tour to promote their new album in their home state of New Jersey. The tour ran from

June through October in venues across the country. It was the Jonas Brothers' longest tour to date.

This tour was also known as the Jonas Brothers' Prom Tour. The concept was to make the concerts like a series of proms on the road. There were prom-related decorations and even photo booths at each concert. The prom theme was fun for the brothers. Since they were homeschooled, they had never had a typical high school prom experience. Now female fans dressed up in prom dresses at their shows.

Second Album Release

On August 7, 2007, the Jonas Brothers' second album hit stores. The promotional work they had done before the release paid off. The album debuted at number five on the Billboard 200 chart. It sold sixty-nine thousand copies in its first week, more than the band's first album had sold in total. The album included several singles that would become hits, like "Hold On," "S.O.S.," and "When You Look Me in the Eyes."

Some critics said the band's music had a bubblegum, teeny-bopper feel. Others, however, recognized the band's potential. "It all adds up [to] an album that's tighter and better than their debut, and one that suggests that they not only deserve their popularity on Radio Disney, but they might have the writing and performing skills to last beyond that as well,"[50] wrote reviewer Stephen Thomas Erlewine.

Teens and tweens fueled the album's popularity. They liked that the band's music was edgier than most Disney performers. Also, the brothers were cute and stylish, and they had fun personalities. This attracted fans, especially young girls, in droves. Fans lined up to buy the album in stores. They downloaded singles on iTunes. Before Disney signed the Jonas Brothers, most Top 40 radio stations would not touch their music. They claimed it was too sugary-sweet for mainstream pop. That changed, however, when tweens swamped radio stations and DJs with phone and e-mail requests to play Jonas Brothers' songs.

Over the following weeks, the album sold consistently. On February 20, 2008, it reached the 1 million sales mark and went

The Story Behind "S.O.S."

A date gone wrong was the inspiration behind the hit single "S.O.S." Nick sat down to write the song after returning home from a terrible night. Nick explains:

I was a bit frustrated because I really liked the girl. I went home and wrote "S.O.S." in about fifteen minutes while sitting on the couch in our family room. I was going through my first real big heartbreak. Originally, it was a song for my ears only so I could get over the pain from the date gone awry and to release my emotions. I had a hunch there was something special about the song, so I first played it for Kevin, who immediately said he was convinced it could be a big hit. I then woke my dad to play the song for him. Despite being a little groggy, he agreed with Kevin. Once we played it for our producer, John Fields, we all hoped it would be a smash. We lucked out because a year later, "S.O.S." was all over the radio.

Joe, Kevin, and Nick Jonas, *Burning Up: On Tour with the Jonas Brothers*. New York: Hyperion, 2008, p. 86.

The Jonas Brothers perform their hit song "S.O.S." at the 2007 American Music Awards.

platinum. Later, the album would go double platinum with sales of over 2 million.

New Format

The album also gathered attention because of its state-of-the-art format. Hollywood Records used the *Jonas Brothers* album to introduce a new format called CDVU+. Along with music the CD had a fifty-page digital booklet with seventy-five photos of the band. In short video clips embedded in photos, the band members talked about songs and demonstrated guitar parts. The CD also had web links and let fans create personalized posters.

Hollywood thought the Jonas Brothers would be the perfect match for the new technology. "We needed a band willing to take a risk, because there are no liner notes and artwork, and it was going to be 100% eco-friendly,"[51] said Hollywood general manager Abbey Konowitch. The Jonas Brothers' young fan base fit perfectly with the new format. Kids in this age group used sites like YouTube and MySpace. They loved learning about their favorite artists online. They also liked lots of pictures and hearing the band members talk. The CDVU+ format gave them exactly what they wanted.

Promotion

As soon as the album hit stores, Disney's promotion efforts grew more intense. The brothers appeared in several high profile spots to increase awareness about the band and build its appeal. They sang at the Miss Teen USA pageant. They also performed at the Disney Channel Games closing ceremonies that aired on television in August.

On August 17 the Jonas Brothers made a guest appearance on the Disney Channel's hit show *Hannah Montana*. The episode aired after the record-breaking premiere of *High School Musical 2*. More than 10 million viewers tuned in for the show. Although the brothers had plenty of experience onstage, this was their first time doing a television sitcom. At the end of the episode, the Jonas Brothers and Hannah Montana joined to sing "We Got the Party."

On August 26 the brothers attended the 2007 Teen Choice Awards. Show organizers recognized the band as a hot new act. They asked the brothers to present an award with *Hannah Montana*'s star, Miley Cyrus. When the brothers stood at the podium with Miley, fans screamed in delight to see them together. The screaming erupted even more when Kevin announced, "We're going to see a lot more of each other this fall because we're going on tour together!"[52]

Touring with Miley

In the fall of 2007, Miley Cyrus was one of Disney's hottest teen stars. She rose to fame on the Disney Channel show *Hannah Montana*. Kids across America loved the sitcom and its likeable lead-

When Disney decided to use the Jonas Brothers as the opening act for Miley Cyrus, the band's career took off.

ing lady. When Disney announced Miley would headline the Best of Both Worlds Tour, fans raced to get tickets. It quickly became the hottest concert event of 2007.

As the opening act for this record-setting tour, Kevin, Nick, and Joe had an incredible opportunity. They would be playing in arenas with the biggest audiences they had ever experienced. "That show, playing the arenas, was a dream come true," said Kevin. "We've been touring for two-and-half years now—playing every little rock 'n' roll club across America, to playing the arenas in those cities."[53]

The band joined Miley for more than fifty concerts from October 2007 through January 2008. At each show the Jonas Brothers rocked their music in front of thousands of screaming fans. They played songs from the new album, mixed in with some older tunes. Nick, Joe, and Kevin set the energy level high in each arena they played. Kids and parents jumped out of their seats, rocking and singing along. Each performance taught the brothers something new. They said it helped them become better entertainers.

During the tour, the boys also became close friends with Miley Cyrus. "It was great," Kevin said. "She really is like a sister so the tour was like one big family on the road. It was a blast."[54]

The tour was so successful that Disney decided to release a 3-D version of the concert in movie theaters. The Jonas Brothers,

Tumble at the American Music Awards

S*ometimes things do not go as planned, even when someone is a teen pop star. At the 2007 American Music Awards, the brothers were ready to perform "S.O.S." The award show had designed three elaborate glass doors onstage. As the music began, the glass would shatter and the brothers would step through the broken glass to center stage. On the night of the show, Joe stepped through his door, but then he tripped and fell. He explains what happened next:*

I'm not really sure where my courage came from, but I wasn't about to let a little slip ruin our night. I jumped to my feet as fast as I could. In my mind, I started thinking about the possible reactions I could have had. Getting up and walking off the stage wasn't an option. I didn't want to look back on this experience with any regret, so I knew I just had to get up and perform with all my heart. Even though I had cut myself badly, I didn't feel any pain. I took all of that adrenaline rushing through my body and made it work for me. I ended up giving one of the best performances of my life.

Joe, Kevin, and Nick Jonas, *Burning Up: On Tour with the Jonas Brothers.* New York: Hyperion, 2008, p. 65.

During the Jonas Brothers' performance at the American Music Awards in 2007, Joe's mishap with a glass door onstage did not interfere with his performance.

as part of the tour, appeared in the movie. In February 2008 the concert movie opened to huge crowds. Another success, it earned close to $70 million at the box office during its run.

Bigger and Better

In the final months of 2007, the Jonas Brothers and Disney moved the band's promotion onto a national stage. The brothers' concert at the Disney Channel Games was such a hit that Disney decided to film another concert, to be shown on television. The boys performed in New York City's Gramercy Park. The special event, titled *The Jonas Brothers in Concert*, premiered on the Disney Channel in October 2007. This time, Kevin, Nick, and Joe were the stars of the show.

Other promotional appearances included performances at the American Music Awards and the Macy's Thanksgiving Day Parade. The band also made appearances on television shows like *Good Morning America*.

With their star rising, the Jonas Brothers rang in 2008 by singing hits "Hold On" and "S.O.S." in New York City for *Dick Clark's New Year's Rockin' Eve*. As host Ryan Seacrest introduced the group, he asked if they thought they could get even bigger in the new year. Little did Seacrest know that the Jonas Brothers were about to do exactly that.

About a week later, the band would be wrapping up its tour with Miley Cyrus. The tour had been such a success that producers decided to extend it two additional months. But Nick, Joe, and Kevin would not be able to join Miley for the additional dates. Instead, the Jonas Brothers were about to embark on their own headlining concert tour.

Chapter 4

Stepping into the Spotlight

The Jonas Brothers had made huge steps toward success in 2007. They had released an album that would eventually go double platinum. Suddenly, it seemed like they were everywhere—the Internet, television, radio, magazine covers, and newspapers. Now the challenge would be carrying their momentum into 2008. Were the brothers finally ready to take a leap into the spotlight? *Billboard* magazine thought so. It picked the group to become the breakout pop touring act of 2008.

Multimillion-Dollar Touring Deal

It would not take long for the band to prove *Billboard* right. On January 3 Live Nation announced a multimillion-dollar, worldwide touring deal with the Jonas Brothers. Live Nation is the world's largest live music company. It has put on global tours for superstar artists like Madonna, the Rolling Stones, and the Police.

Even though the brothers had never headlined a major tour before, Live Nation signed them to a long-term deal. The Jonas Brothers would play more than 140 concerts in arenas and theaters over the next two years. "This band creates pandemonium wherever they go. They sell out dates instantly and always leave their loyal fans wanting more. We couldn't be more thrilled to be partners with them on their journey to superstardom,"[55] said Bruce Kapp, Live Nation's senior vice president of touring.

Nick, Joe, and Kevin were thrilled about signing with Live Nation. They issued a statement saying: "The level of commitment and passion that everyone at Live Nation has shown for our band has been inspiring. Together we are going to bring our show to millions of fans around the world. We couldn't be more excited about our future together."[56]

Look Me in the Eyes Tour

Live Nation also announced the brothers would be immediately headlining a new tour. It was called the Look Me in the Eyes Tour, named after their latest single. In only a few weeks, the tour would kick off in Tucson, Arizona. The brothers would play thirty-nine shows across the country, finishing up in March.

When tickets went on sale, fans rewarded Live Nation's faith in the Jonas Brothers. The shows sold out dates in every city. Several cities added new dates or changed their venue to fit in more

The boys' concerts began to sell out in minutes, and the band created fan pandemonium wherever they played, as shown here at the May 2008 Wango Tango concert in Irvine, California.

fans. In Los Angeles the brothers set a new record at the Gibson Amphitheater by selling out their show in two minutes. It was the fastest sellout in the amphitheater's thirty-six year history.

The brothers were excited to headline their own tour. "I really don't know what to expect. This next tour is going to be very interesting. The first leg sold out, and we're completely surprised and shocked,"[57] said Joe. They were also amazed at their fans' overwhelming response and support. "Day in and day out, we're always freaking out. We always hoped, but we never really expected that we would be able to be in a place where we could do those things. It's unbelievably awesome,"[58] said Kevin.

On the final night of the tour, the brothers played at the Izod Center in East Rutherford, New Jersey, near their hometown of Wyckoff. Fans, family, and friends packed the arena for the show. "We used to go to the Izod Center as kids, and whenever we drove into Manhattan, we had to pass right by it. 'One day we'll play there,' we always said to each other. Now here we were—and not only were we about to play there, we had sold it out! It was incredible!"[59] said the brothers.

After the show, the brothers celebrated with close family and friends at Planet Hollywood in New York City. Their first headlining tour was a success. "That night in New Jersey was the end of our tour, but it was also the

The boys play an acoustic set for the opening night of their successful 2008 Look Me in the Eyes Tour.

beginning of something amazing. It was the start of who we're going to be for years to come,"[60] said the brothers.

Media Blitz

The brothers also continued their media blitz. They appeared in magazines and television shows. Radio Disney interviewed the boys regularly. On January 21, 2008, they appeared on *The Ellen DeGeneres Show*. The talk show host asked how they kept getting bigger and bigger. "Our amazing fans. I think its word of mouth. Every single time one person listens to the CD, they pass it to a friend or tell them about it and I think it's just grown from there,"[61] Kevin answered.

On April 24, 2008, the entire Jonas family, including Denise, Kevin Sr., and Frankie, appeared on *The Oprah Winfrey Show*.

Fashion Frenzy

In addition to their music, the Jonas Brothers are also known for their sophisticated sense of style. Stylist Michelle Tomaszewski has worked with the brothers since the end of 2006. According to Tomaszewski:

> Even though they're brothers, they really like to stand out as being individuals. I think it's important for them to stand out, but . . . they are a band so it still has to look like there's a common thread. Kevin . . . likes to definitely wear the more fashionable clothes. He likes to kind of be a little bit more grown up in the way he dresses. Joe . . . likes to take a little bit more risk in what he wears. He'll wear a bright color and he wears it really well. Purple is not really a masculine color, but Joe makes it masculine. It's strange how you put a color on Joe that you wouldn't think would look good on a guy and he wears it well. And then, there's Nick. He's the old soul, but he's the youngest. He definitely has a more gentlemanly feel about him. Even though he looks fashionable, he's more serene about the way he looks. Each stands out with their personality, and I think that's what makes them look good.

Quoted in Natalie Broulette, "The Jonas Brothers' Stylist Talks Fashion and the Grammys," Film.com, February 5, 2009. www.film.com/celebrities/jonas-brothers/story/jonas-brothers-stylist-talks-fashion/25900544.

Thousands of fans had sent e-mails, made phone calls, and started online petitions asking Oprah to invite the Jonas Brothers on her talk show. Some even posted their pleas to Oprah on YouTube. Oprah called the Jonas Brothers "the most requested guests ever" on her show.

Family First

The Jonas Brothers were fast becoming the hottest boy band on the planet. Handling so much fame as teenagers was not easy. Yet the Jonas Brothers did not let their success go to their heads.

Everyone who met the brothers noted how incredibly grounded and down-to-earth they were. They were teen superstars but still acted as if they could be the boys next door.

The brothers give their parents credit for keeping them grounded amid all the craziness. Kevin Sr. serves as the band's comanager, and both parents have been very hands-on in the brothers' careers. "We have our amazing family around us," said Kevin. "Our parents taught us that when you are at the top, work like you are at the bottom, and we try to live like that."[62]

Kevin, Joe, and Nick believe that family is the most important thing in their lives. They enjoy an open relationship with each other and their parents. They can talk to their parents about anything without feeling embarrassed or afraid. Being involved in

The Jonases, a close-knit and open family, travel and live together when the boys are on tour.

the boys' lives has always been important to Kevin Sr. and Denise. "It's very important to us that they can live their dreams but the first priority to us is that they're good people,"[63] said Kevin Sr.

The family seizes moments together whenever they can. The six Jonases travel together on one tour bus. They also try to make birthday celebrations fun, even if they are on the road. "What I think has been so fabulous for us is that we've remained as a family unit and been able to be intact as a family," said Denise. "And I've been able to be mom in their life and their dad's there."[64]

The boys may be superstars, but they have family chores like any other teenagers. According to Nick, his parents will take away privileges like cell phones and television if they slack off on their chores. "At the end of the day, like you get off stage of a really big show, Mom's going to make you clean your bunk,"[65] said Nick.

Brothers Together

Kevin, Joe, and Nick are also very close with each other. "We're each other's best friends," said Kevin. "People ask us, 'Do you guys fight?' But, really, we get along so well."[66] Although they do not fight, there are some disagreements. Joe says that they bicker "over small things, like who's going to play video games first when we get to a venue. And sometimes you see a very pretty girl in the audience and you think, 'I hope she's a fan of me,' and then you realize that she's Nick's fan—because she's holding a sign that says, 'Nick, look at me,' or 'Nick, I'm your wife and you just don't know it.' And you're like, 'Oh bummer.'"[67]

The brothers lean on each other for support when life as pop stars gets crazy. "The good thing is that we have each other," said Nick. "On the road, Joe and I share a room, so we'll have conversations where we're in our beds and talk until 2:00 in the morning. We just have that relationship where we're really able to talk about anything."[68]

Burning Up

Before their first headline tour finished, the Jonas Brothers announced they would be heading out on tour again. The Burning Up Tour would kick off on July 4 in Toronto and run through September. The boys would also be joining Avril Lavigne's European tour for sixteen shows in June. "We've had an awesome time touring and having an opportunity to see so many of our fans. Every time we play, we learn so much and grow both as artists and a band. We really can't wait to get back on the road this summer,"[69] the brothers said.

Before each show the brothers have a routine that helps them get ready to take the stage. About forty-five minutes before showtime, they go into lockdown. No one is allowed into their dressing room. They practice, warm up their voices, stretch, and think about the show. Five minutes before showtime, they gather with family and friends in a circle for prayer. At the end of the prayer, everyone gets excited, puts their hands in the middle of the circle, and shouts, "Living the dream! Living the dream!"

After a show, the brothers might be tired and sweaty, but they also feel like they have accomplished something. They like to take a few minutes to cool down and unwind from using so much energy onstage. Then they get ready to do it all again the next night.

Reality Television

During the Look Me in the Eyes Tour, Disney filmed the band for a reality television show. *Jonas Brothers: Living the Dream* gave fans an inside look at the band's life on the road. Fifteen episodes aired during the summer of 2008. The episodes showed rehearsals, performances, and pieces of the brothers' personal lives.

Camp Rock

Disney also asked the brothers to show off their acting skills in a new made-for-television movie called *Camp Rock*. At first Disney executives were only interested in having Joe star in the movie. That did not sit well with the brothers, and they declined the project. When Disney rewrote the script to include parts for Kevin and Nick, the Jonas Brothers agreed to film the movie.

In the movie the brothers play a pop rock band called Connect 3. When Joe's character, Shane Grey, lets fame go to his head, his bandmates send him back to the place where they first got together, Camp Rock. This is a summer camp where teens practice and share music and performing skills. While at camp Shane meets down-to-earth Mitchie Torres, played by Demi Lovato, who helps him regain his passion for music.

Of course the movie features music from the Jonas Brothers. They performed together for the song "Play My Music." Joe sang a solo ballad and a duet with costar Demi. All three joined the entire cast to sing the *Camp Rock* anthem, "We Rock."

Joe was excited to play the part of Shane Grey. "I had a phone call with the director and he told me about the character and right away I was very into the movie. I really wanted to do it," Joe said. "My character is a pop star who kind of loses his way and has to go back to his roots. And he's kind of a jerk so he's gotta grow out of that. It was fun to play him because I'm definitely not a jerk, so playing a jerk in the movie definitely, you know, it stretches me a little bit but I really enjoyed it."[70]

Fitting the movie into their busy schedule was a challenge. The brothers ended up filming their scenes in increments at the movie's remote location near Toronto, Canada. They traveled back and forth to the set between performances at sold-out shows and while recording their third album.

On June 20, 2008, *Camp Rock* premiered on the Disney Channel. More than 9 million viewers watched, making it an instant hit. Fans loved the music and rushed out to buy the soundtrack. The movie was so successful that a sequel was planned to begin filming in summer 2009 with a 2010 release date. Insiders report that Nick and Kevin will have bigger roles in the new film, and the youngest Jonas, Frankie, will make an appearance.

While filming *Camp Rock* the brothers became close friends with costar Demi, who was one of Disney's newest teen stars. A

While filming Camp Rock, *the brothers became close friends with Disney costar Demi Lovato, who would later become the opening act for the boys' Burning Up Tour.*

powerful singer, Demi joined the brothers on their Burning Up Tour as the opening act. They also cowrote six songs on her debut album. Demi said:

> Some days I would have an idea on piano and we'd start writing the chords. Everyone had an equal amount of input, which was awesome. It's not like two people are writing and someone punches in a line. It was a real collaboration and I don't think I've ever experienced anything like that. It was awesome. I love writing with them and they're so completely professional.[71]

Recording on the Road

After the band's second album was released in 2007, the Jonas Brothers immediately started writing songs for the next one. Unfortunately, the band was touring and did not have time to go to the studio to record. Nick explained:

> We met with our managers and we said "Where can we record these songs, because we're going to be so busy?" So they retrofitted a Gibson guitar bus to be a studio, and they brought it out and our producer John Fields started work-

White House Easter Egg Roll

One of the Jonas Brothers' favorite memories was performing at the annual White House Easter egg–rolling contest. They were all excited to meet President George W. Bush and First Lady Laura Bush. What did the president think of the band? According to the guys, President Bush must be a fan, because he leaned over with a wink and whispered the title of one of their songs, "That's just the way we roll."

ing on the road. We did that for about two weeks on the bus, and then we went into the studio for about a week after that for a couple last things, and then the record was done.[72]

A Little Bit Longer

The new album, titled *A Little Bit Longer*, demonstrated the increasing maturity of the band. "I think we grew up on the road a little bit. It's not like we were immature and now we're changing our sound or anything like that, but we're getting older and I think we've learned more from life in the last couple of years,"[73] said Joe. On the album the brothers again drew on personal experiences to inspire their songs. In fact, the title track, "A Little Bit Longer," is a song that Nick wrote about dealing with diabetes. The album also included other hit singles like "Burnin' Up" and "Tonight."

Of all the album's songs, Nick was most proud of "Lovebug." He says:

> In my opinion, "Lovebug" is probably the best song we've recorded to date. It's different from a lot of the other ones we've written. It's about that feeling you get when you fall in love after recovering from a breakup. Just when you thought you'd never have those feelings again, along comes someone who rocks your world. We took a risk with it by incorporating all sorts of devices that were unusual choices for us, such as talking and using unique musical instruments. . . . We had a vision of how that song sounded in our heads and recorded it exactly that way.[74]

A Little Bit Longer hit stores on August 12, 2008. The band was in New York City for the release and decided to make a midnight trip to Virgin Megastore to pick up a copy. Screaming fans filled the streets. Although it was August the brothers said they felt like they were in Times Square on New Year's Eve.

Overwhelming fan support helped *A Little Bit Longer* debut at number one on the Billboard 200. It sold more than 525,000 copies in its first week. The album would eventually sell more than a million copies and go platinum. That same week the Jonas

Brothers achieved another industry first. The band's third album held the number one spot in the Nielsen SoundScan Top 10. The *Camp Rock* soundtrack was number eight, and the band's second album jumped a few spots to number ten. It was the first time any artist held three spots in the Top 10.

Romantic Rumors

As the brothers grew more famous, fans and media speculated about their love lives. Much to their amusement, the brothers quickly became tabloid material. "The media like to take our pictures. So if we're with friends, and they're female, we're immediately dating. . . . And we find out that we're dating people that we've never met before all the time—because [the press] knows what kind of audience we have, and they like to stir up controversy,"[75] said Joe.

Nick and Miley

One of the biggest rumors swirled around Nick and teen queen Miley Cyrus. The two were rumored to be dating, but both denied it in the press. "There was a point in our lives when we were very close. We were neighbors when we were on tour together. It was good. Just really close. But it would crack me up—I would read these stories online, people saying things that were completely untrue,"[76] said Nick.

Eventually, Miley Cyrus confirmed their relationship and breakup in an interview with *Seventeen* magazine. "We became boyfriend and girlfriend the day we met. . . . Nick and I loved each other," Miley said. "We still do, but we were in love with each other. For two years he was basically my 24/7. But it was really hard to keep it from people. We were arguing a lot, and it really wasn't fun."[77] According to Miley, the couple split at the end of 2007, and she took the breakup hard.

In 2008 the tabloids linked Nick to Selena Gomez, star of Disney's *Wizards of Waverly Place* sitcom. Selena had appeared in the band's "Burnin' Up" video and was good friends with Demi Lovato. Although Nick and Selena denied dating, the rumors appeared con-

Nick and Miley Cyrus appear onstage in late 2007. The two were in a romantic relationship that lasted almost two years.

firmed when each told a similar dating story in different interviews. Nick told his version: "On one date, the girl said to me, 'I don't kiss on the first date.' So I said, 'I don't follow the rules.'"[78]

Joe's Romantic Troubles

In the summer of 2008 Joe and country singer Taylor Swift were tagged as a couple, but neither confirmed the relationship. When it went sour in the fall, Taylor talked about the breakup on *The*

Ellen DeGeneres Show. She said that Joe dumped her over the phone. She also claimed to have written the song "Forever and Always" about their breakup.

In response, Joe posted a letter to fans online, in which he said:

> Several things I will state with all my heart. . . . I never cheated on a girlfriend. It might make someone feel better to assume or imply I have been unfaithful but it is simply not true. Maybe there were reasons for a breakup. Maybe the heart moved on. Perhaps feelings changed. . . . I called to discuss feelings with the other person. . . . Those feelings were obviously not well received. I did not end the conversation. Someone else did. Phone calls can only last as long as the person on the other end of the line is willing to talk.[79]

While filming the band's "Lovebug" video, Joe met actress Camilla Belle on the set. Although he preferred not to talk about his dating life, friends admitted that Joe and Camilla had quietly dated after his breakup with Taylor. By July 2009, however, Joe and Camilla's romance fizzled, and her media representative confirmed that the pair had split.

Kevin has not escaped romantic rumors either. In July 2009 Kevin became engaged to his girlfriend of two years, Danielle Deleasa. Unlike his brothers, Kevin did not meet Danielle while touring or in Hollywood. They met on vacation with family in the Bahamas.

Winning Awards

In the past the Jonas Brothers had presented awards to other artists. In 2008, however, they were nominated for and winning awards themselves. In March the band won the Kids' Choice Award for Best Musical Group. At the Teen Choice Awards in August, the brothers arrived in coordinated Ray-Ban sunglasses to the delight of screaming fans. They were one of the night's biggest winners, taking home six awards, including Breakout Group. The Jonas Brothers also earned a nomination for MTV's Video Music Awards for their "Burnin' Up" video. While they did not win, they performed live at the Video Music Awards in September.

In November the brothers returned to the American Music Awards and performed their single "Tonight." This time they did not leave the show empty-handed. Kevin, Nick, and Joe were thrilled to take home the T-Mobile Breakthrough Artist Award.

Wrapping Up 2008

As 2008 ended the Jonas Brothers performed "Tonight," "Love-bug," and "Burnin' Up" at the halftime show of the Dallas Cowboys' annual Thanksgiving Day game. They joined other celebrities for the annual tree-lighting ceremony in New York City's Rockefeller Center. They also returned to New York for another performance on *Dick Clark's New Year's Rockin' Eve*.

The past twelve months had been an incredible journey for Kevin, Nick, and Joe. *Forbes* magazine named the Jonas Brothers as the Breakout Stars of 2008. With sold-out tours, successful albums, and screaming fans, the brothers' hard work was finally paying off. Now they looked forward to new challenges and opportunities in 2009.

Chapter 5

Living the Dream

The Jonas Brothers entered 2009 with big expectations. Within two years they had gone from virtual unknowns to one of the hottest bands in the world. Fans could not get enough of everything Jonas. And the brothers were prepared to give them even more. They had a new 3-D movie, book, album, tour, and television show in the works. With so many projects, Kevin, Nick, and Joe's hectic schedule was not slowing down anytime soon.

The whirlwind kicked off in January when the brothers joined the inaugural festivities for newly elected President Barack Obama. They performed the night before the inauguration at the Kids' Inaugural Ball. They also visited the White House on inauguration night. As a surprise they waited for First Daughters Sasha and Malia Obama and their friends at the end of a scavenger hunt. Once the girls discovered them, the brothers played acoustic songs and posed for pictures.

2009 Grammys

The world spun even faster when the 2009 Grammy nominations were announced. To their delight the Jonas Brothers earned a nomination for Best New Artist. Past artists who have won the award include the Beatles, Alicia Keys, and Carrie Underwood. The brothers were thrilled to be nominated for one of the music industry's highest honors. "As an artist and a songwriter . . . you always dream about being nominated for a Grammy,"[80] said Nick.

As the award show approached, the brothers were excited and nervous. Along with their nomination they were also performing live at the show. The thrill of a lifetime came when Grammy producers decided to pair the brothers with Stevie Wonder. The music legend had been an idol and inspiration for the brothers for years. Now they would have the chance to perform with him on music's biggest stage.

On February 8, 2009, the brothers arrived at the fifty-first annual Grammy awards in Los Angeles. Looking sharp in tuxedos, they posed on the red carpet with other celebrities before heading into the show.

First Lady Michelle Obama (far right) and daughters Malia (center) and Sasha (hidden) watch the Jonas Brothers perform at the Kids' Inaugural Concert on January 19, 2009.

For the brothers, however, the night's highlight was their performance with Wonder. With Wonder at keyboards, the brothers sang "Burnin' Up" with him for the Grammy audience. As the first song ended, the four performers immediately bridged the music into Wonder's hit "Superstition." It was an amazing moment for the brothers. Not only did they get to sing one of Wonder's classics, he had agreed to sing on one of their songs. In fact, they were amazed to learn that Wonder already had "Burnin' Up" on his iPod.

Some critics blasted show producers for teaming Wonder with the Jonas Brothers. They called it an odd pairing and an awkward moment. Still, others pointed out that Wonder had also entered the music industry years before as a hot teen artist.

To the brothers it did not matter what critics said. "Performing with Stevie was like the highlight of the century," said Joe. While they lost out to British artist Adele for the Best New Artist Grammy, they considered the night a success. "Although we didn't win Best New Artist, I think for us the win was the performance with Stevie because he's one of our idols,"[81] Nick said.

Moving onto the Big Screen

In February 2009 the brothers made the leap onto the silver screen. On the 2008 Burning Up Tour, Disney executives filmed concerts and behind-the-scenes footage for a new movie, *Jonas Brothers: The 3D Concert Experience*.

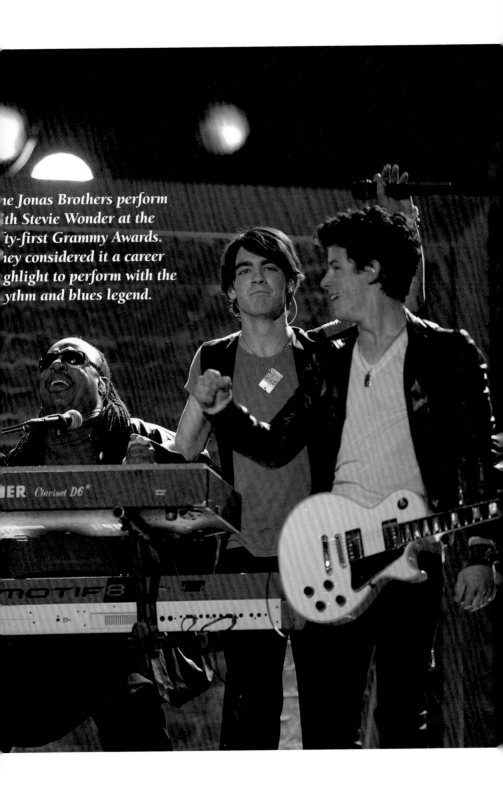

The Jonas Brothers perform with Stevie Wonder at the fifty-first Grammy Awards. They considered it a career highlight to perform with the rhythm and blues legend.

The Jonas Brothers' movie was modeled after the hugely successful Hannah Montana 3-D concert movie. "We're really excited about shooting these guys in 3-D, they play an amazing show with a lot of physical stunts,"[82] said producer Art Repola. The movie's director, Bruce Hendricks, used different cameras to put fans both in the front row of the concert and onstage with the band. He filmed movie segments as if viewers were at the show as a musician, a background singer, or sharing a microphone with one of the brothers.

The movie debuted on February 27, 2009, with massive hype. The opening scenes showed girls chasing the brothers, much like the Beatles' classic movie *A Hard Day's Night*. The movie featured the brothers performing hits like "Burnin' Up," "S.O.S.," and "Hold On." They also performed with teen stars Taylor Swift and Demi Lovato. In between concert footage the movie shifted to behind-the-scenes glimpses of the brothers' lives. During the film's opening weekend, the brothers delighted viewers and traveled to theaters around the country to meet fans.

Unfortunately, the movie was not the home run that the studio had anticipated. It brought in a disappointing $12.7 million during opening weekend. The film did not even take the number one spot of the weekend. Critics called the Jonas Brothers' movie a flop. They questioned if the band's popularity was waning.

World Tour

Two weeks after their disappointing movie release, however, the brothers came roaring back. They announced the Jonas Brothers World Tour 2009. The new tour would take the band to three continents with dates in North and South America and Europe. The tour would also feature music from their upcoming fourth album.

This would be the band's most ambitious tour yet. Producers designed an enormous 140-foot (42.7m) stage in the center of the arena. They also filled the concert with special effects and cutting-edge technology. "This tour is going to be about really connecting with our fans," said Joe. "We've got new music that's taking us in new directions plus a mind-blowing production that's

A Day on the Road

So, what is a day on the road like for the Jonas Brothers? Most of the time it can be pretty hectic. Sometimes the brothers get up as early as 4 A.M. They head out for interviews with newspapers and magazines. Next they might ride to a radio station to talk live on the air with the disc jockey. If they have a show that night, the brothers do a sound check around 3 P.M. Then they get ready for the show. After the show is over, their day might not be done. Sometimes there are more media interviews that last late into the night! Finally, the guys hop on the bus to travel to their next stop. Amid all the craziness they do manage to squeeze in some time for meals. It might be room service in a hotel or cereal on the bus, but the brothers make sure they eat well so they have the energy for a great show each night.

going to surprise everyone. We want to give the audience the summer concert they're not going to ever forget."[83]

The Jonas Brothers smashed any doubts about their popularity when concert tickets went on sale. Within minutes many cities sold out. In the first weekend the concerts sold an incredible eight hundred thousand tickets in North America. Tremendous fan demand in the New York area sold out five arena shows. "Ticket sales for this tour have been phenomenal," said Jason Garner, chief executive officer of global music for Live Nation. "The band has already sold out arena dates in 13 major cities, including Madrid, London and Paris. . . . It's clear to us that Jonas Brothers are a true global touring powerhouse."[84]

Fans Come First

The Jonas Brothers credit their fans for driving their popularity and success. "We have the most amazing fans in the world. We'd be nowhere without them,"[85] said Kevin. During shows the band feeds off the crowd's energy. The brothers say that fans are what

The Jonas Brothers have quickly developed a loyal fan base willing to wait in line to purchase tickets for their performances.

turn a good show into a great one. As a thank-you, the Jonas Brothers have been known to surprise fans waiting in line for tickets and play a few songs. They also frequently pick fans out of the "nosebleed" seats and bring them down into the front rows. Sometimes they hold ticket lotteries for the first twenty rows of seats to make sure dedicated fans can get access to great seats.

The brothers also work hard at fan meet-and-greet events. While some celebrities go through the motions, the Jonas Brothers truly enjoy meeting their fans. At one Dallas event they stood in 99°F (37°C) heat to greet over four hundred fans. "They are the new music business, work hard, touch your fans,"[86] said Brad Wavra, Live Nation vice president.

The brothers also take an active role online. They blog on MySpace, post behind-the-scenes videos on YouTube, and frequently update their Web site. Even during shows they encourage fans to take pictures and videos on their cell phones and then upload them online. "When it came to the live show, when we saw cameras or cell phones or camera phones, it was never anything that concerned us. We really viewed it as something that was going to expand the boys' reach,"[87] said band manager Phil McIntyre.

Crazy Moments

Sometimes, however, the fans can get a bit out of control. Some have thrown underwear and lip gloss onstage. Girls regularly chase the boys, trying to get autographs or pictures. A line of cars frequently follows their tour bus. Fans swerve and honk, trying to get the brothers' attention.

What was one of the craziest fan moments? Kevin recalls:

One time, we were on vacation in the Bahamas and we were at dinner as a family and this mother came up to the manager of the restaurant and said she wanted to go surprise her sons who were in the back—the Jonas Brothers. Meanwhile, we were at dinner with our mom! So this woman was lying about being our mother to try and come back and get her daughters to take a picture with us. We had a good laugh about that one! I think we really do appreciate the effort that the fans make to try to get backstage and things like that. We are very flattered by it. They have very unique and amazing ways of showing their appreciation for us.[88]

Giving Back

From the beginning Kevin, Nick, and Joe have believed that life is more than writing and performing music. They feel lucky to have a supportive family and the opportunity to pursue their dreams. They also know that many people are not so fortunate. As a child on Broadway, Nick saw homeless families on the streets of New York as he traveled to rehearsals and performances. Seeing their hardships inspired Nick to start the Nicholas Jonas Change for the Children Foundation in 2002. The foundation's mission was to help poor, homeless, and terminally ill kids.

When Kevin and Joe joined Nick in the band, they also wanted a role in helping others. Nick's foundation became the Change for the Children Foundation (www.changeforthechildren.org). Today it supports several children's charities. "We started the Jonas Brothers' Change for the Children Foundation to support programs that motivate and inspire children to face adversity with confidence, determination and the will to succeed. When we started the foundation, we figured the best people to help children are their peers—kids helping other kids who are a little less fortunate,"[89] said the brothers.

In August 2008 Bayer announced that Nick Jonas had agreed to become a "diabetes ambassador" for Bayer Diabetes Care. Together they will provide resources and information for young people to help them manage diabetes. "Nearly every day I hear from someone like me who says that I make them feel it's OK to have diabetes and that's really cool that I can do that," said Nick. "I know I'm lucky because I have a family that encourages me a lot. I want to give that same inspiration to other kids with diabetes, and working with Bayer lets me do that."[90]

In addition, the brothers spend time playing charity concerts. They joined Miley Cyrus in September 2008 for a concert benefiting the City of Hope in Los Angeles. In January 2009 they gave a concert at the 2009 Charity Preview before the North American International Auto Show. Some shows are smaller, but no less important. In October 2007 the band played in a nine-hundred-seat auditorium to raise money for a local elementary school's playground for kids with special needs.

A Fourth Album

In 2009 the Jonas Brothers were also hard at work on their fourth album, titled *Lines, Vines, and Trying Times*. "The title is a bit of poetry we came up with on the set for the TV show," said Nick. "Lines are something that someone feeds you, whether it's good or bad. Vines are the things that get in the way of the path that you're on, and trying times—well, obviously we're younger guys, but we're aware of what's going on in the world and we're trying to bring some light to it."[91]

The album was released on June 15, 2009. Many people wondered if this album would help the brothers make the transition from a teen boy band to adult musicians. "It definitely is a progression in our music and a growth for us. We're very excited about this new album. . . . There's more to the music rather than just a typical kind of relationship song,"[92] said Joe.

Television Stars

In May 2009 the Jonas Brothers launched another new project. Their television show *JONAS* premiered on the Disney Channel. In the show the brothers play a fictional rock band of brothers who are trying to live a normal life in spite of their fame. "We've tried to create a fusion of a sitcom and a music video and use original Jonas Brothers songs as the foundation to glue it together,"[93] said Gary Marsh, entertainment president of Disney Channels Worldwide.

Working on their own sitcom was a new challenge for the brothers. For Nick, the transition to television acting was hard. "I'm kind of a perfectionist. I'm very hard on myself when it comes to acting. In real life I have a very dry sense of humor and sometimes I can't master that on camera. I'm still learning,"[94] Nick said.

Keeping It Real

Through all the craziness, the Jonas Brothers have managed to remain wholesome, hardworking young men. As evangelical Christians, faith is important to them. Even on the road, the family always finds time to pray and worship together.

Part of the Jonas Brothers' appeal to teens and parents is their old-fashioned values. The brothers steer away from temptations like smoking, alcohol, and drugs. They also wear silver rings on their left-hand ring fingers. Although they are sometimes reluc-

The Jonas Brothers answer questions from the press about their newest effort, the Disney Channel show JONAS, which premiered in May 2009.

tant to talk about the rings, Nick said, "To us, the rings are a constant reminder to live a life of values. It's about being a gentleman, treating people with respect and being the best guys we can be."[95]

Looking Ahead

The future looks bright for the Jonas Brothers. Only time will tell if they can successfully make the leap from teen stars to adult celebrities. Many people believe that they have a good chance. Kevin, Nick, and Joe are not just pretty faces thrown onstage to sing. They have the talent to write their own songs, play their own instruments, and perform. And they have undeniable appeal. "They sell. They sell magazines, they sell concert tickets, they sell albums, they sell videos, they sell merchandise," said Brad Wavra, Live Nation vice president. "Every guy on the planet wants to get a taste of this band."[96]

Many wonder if the brothers will stay together as a band or if they will strike out on their own. For now, the brothers insist they will stick together. "We all have dreams of our own, sure," Joe said. "But a band is a band. We're in it together."[97] They might branch out into writing songs for other groups, like they have for

Fun on Tour

So what do the guys do for fun when they are on tour? When they can catch a spare moment, the brothers try to head out to a local golf course. Each of them loves to play golf. The quiet and peace on the course helps them relax a bit from their hectic schedules. Sometimes Kevin Sr. or other tour members join them on the course. The Jonas Brothers also like to bowl and play baseball and football, sometimes in the parking lot of the arena where they are performing.

Also, when they have a few extra hours, Kevin, Nick, and Joe like to see other groups perform. They enjoy listening to other people's music and keeping on top of trends. Listening to other creative artists inspires the Jonas Brothers to work even harder.

pal Demi Lovato. Or they might try more acting. Whatever the opportunity, they are ready to face it together.

Despite their quick rise to fame and fortune, Kevin, Nick, and Joe want fans to know that success has not changed them. "We're really a lot like you. We're not an 'act,' we're just three brothers from New Jersey who are living our dream."[98]

Introduction: The Right Mix

1. Quoted in Jocelyn Vena, "Jonas Brothers and 'Twilight' Rule the Kids' Choice Awards," MTV.com, March 28, 2009. www.mtv.com/news/articles/1608034/20090328/jonas_brothers.jhtml.

2. Quoted in Vena, "Jonas Brothers and 'Twilight' Rule the Kids' Choice Awards."

3. Quoted in Gina Scarpa, "The Jonas Brothers Star in Disney Reality Series," BuddyTV, March 21, 2008. www.buddytv.com/articles/jonas-brothers-living-the-dream/the-jonas-brothers-star-in-dis-17854.aspx.

Chapter 1: Musical Beginnings

4. Quoted in *Life Story Magazine: Jonas Love Issue*, "For the Love of Music," 2009, p. 90.

5. Quoted in *Life Story Magazine: Jonas Love Issue*, "For the Love of Music," p. 90.

6. Quoted in Sean Patrick Reily, "It's Full Scream Ahead for the Jonas Brothers," *Los Angeles Times*, February 26, 2009. http://latimesblogs.latimes.com/music_blog/2009/02/the-jonas-broth.html.

7. Quoted in Suzanne Hadley, "Star Bright," *Clubhouse*, www.clubhousemagazine.com/truelife/interviews/a0001236.cfm.

8. Quoted in *Life Story Magazine: Jonas Love Issue*, "For the Love of Music," p. 90.

9. Quoted in Jason Gay, "The Clean Teen Machine," *Rolling Stone*, August 7, 2008. www.rollingstone.com/news/story/21896731/the_clean_teen_machine/print.

10. Quoted in YouTube, "Jonas Brothers E! True Hollywood Story Young Hollywood Story, Episode HQ [Part 1]." www.youtube.com/watch?v=CHOFE0oDJGI.

11. Quoted in Charles Dickens, *A Christmas Carol*, Project Gutenberg. EBook. www.gutenberg.org/files/46/46-h/46-h.htm#5.

12. Quoted in Hadley, "Star Bright."

13. Quoted in Gay, "The Clean Teen Machine."

14. Quoted in *Life Story Magazine: Jonas Love Issue*, "For the Love of Music," pp. 90-91.

15. Quoted in Claire Askew, "Band Interview: The Jonas Brothers, on the Road, Promoting Their First CD," Ken Phillips Publicity Group. www.kenphillipsgroup.com/Phillips/jb kansascitystar.htm.

16. Quoted in Daylight/Columbia Records, "The Jonas Brothers Back on the Road for American Club Tour," Ken Phillips Publicity Group, January 20, 2006. www.kenphillipsgroup .com/Phillips/jonasbrothers.htm.

17. Quoted in Mike Rimmer, "Jonas Brothers: It's These Guys, Not Busted, Who Hit in the US with 'Year 3000,'" *Cross Rhythms*, June 28, 2007. www.crossrhythms.co.uk/articles/ music/Jonas_Brothers_Its_these_guys_not_Busted_who_hit _in_the_US_with_Year_3000/27777/p1.

18. Quoted in Ken Phillips Publicity Group, "The Jonas Brothers." www.kenphillipsgroup.com/Phillips/jonasbrothers .htm.

19. Quoted in *Life Story Magazine: Jonas Love Issue*, "For the Love of Music," p. 91.

20. Quoted in Homeschool.com, "Homeschool.com's Interview with Denise Jonas," 2009. www.homeschool.com/Teleconfer ence/JonasBrothers2009/default.asp.

21. Quoted in Kim Jones, "INO Records Signs 12-Year-Old Singer/Actor Nicholas Jonas," About.com. http://christian music.about.com/od/upcomingreleases/a/aanjonassigned.htm.

22. Nicholas Jonas, "Letter from Nicholas Jonas," INO Records.com. www.inorecords.com/nicholasjonas/nj-letter.html.

23. Kevin Jonas, "Letter from Pastor Kevin Jonas," INO Records .com. www.inorecords.com/nicholasjonas/kj-letter.html.

Chapter 2: Band of Brothers

24. Quoted in Mikael Wood, "Patience Pays Off," *Billboard*, February 24, 2007, p. 57.

25. Quoted in Wood, "Patience Pays Off."

26. Quoted in *Life Story Magazine: Jonas Love Issue*, "For the Love of Music," p. 91.

27. Quoted in Tom Campisi, "Jonas Brothers Return to Christian School Alma Mater for Sold-Out Shows," *Good News Daily*, May 2, 2007. www.goodnewsdaily.net/modules/news/article.php?storyid=4882.

28. Quoted in Rimmer, "Jonas Brothers."

29. Quoted in Daylight/Columbia Records, "Jonas Brothers Back on the Road for American Club Tour," PR Newswire, January 20, 2006. www.prnewswire.com/cgi-bin/stories.pl?ACCT=104&STORY=/www/story/01-20-2006/0004264222&EDATE=.

30. Quoted in *Life Story Magazine: Jonas Love Issue*, "For the Love of Music," p. 92.

31. Quoted in *Life Story Magazine: Jonas Love Issue*, "Putting Heart & Soul into Every Performance," 2009, p. 37.

32. Quoted in John Moser, "The Jonas Brothers: Heartthrobs of the Hanson Kind," *Allentown (PA) Morning Call*, February 18, 2006. www.kenphillipsgroup.com/Phillips/jballentown.htm.

33. Quoted in Gay, "The Clean Teen Machine."

34. Quoted in Diabetes Research Institute Foundation, "Nick Jonas Reveals He Has Diabetes," news release, March 14, 2007. www.childrenwithdiabetes.com/pressreleases/dri20070311.htm.

35. Quoted in YouTube, "Jonas Brothers E! True Hollywood Story Young Hollywood Story, Episode HQ [Part 2]." www.youtube.com/watch?v=NLCrSv1rywY.

36. Quoted in Patrick Ferrucci, "Brothers in Arms," *New Haven (CT) Register*, February 16, 2006. www.overflow.essential-ink.com/Phillips/jbctcentral.htm.

37. Quoted in Ken Phillips Publicity Group, "The Jonas Brothers."

38. Quoted in Askew, "Band Interview."

39. Quoted in Askew, "Band Interview."

40. Quoted in Katy Kroll, "Perseverance Pays Off on Charts for Sibling Trio," *Billboard*, August 23, 2006. www.billboard.com/bbcom/esearch/article_display.jsp?vnu_content_id=1003052442.

41. Quoted in Wood, "Patience Pays Off."

42. Quoted in Gay, "The Clean Teen Machine."

Chapter 3: Joining the Disney Family

43. Quoted in Wood, "Patience Pays Off."

44. Quoted in PR Newswire, "The Jonas Brothers Sign Record Deal with Disney's Hollywood Records," February 8, 2007. http://sev.prnewswire.com/entertainment/20070208/LATH 11608022007-1.html.

45. Quoted in Wood, "Patience Pays Off."

46. Quoted in PR Newswire, "The Jonas Brothers Sign Record Deal with Disney's Hollywood Records."

47. Quoted in Jonathan Widran, "Hot Teen Group the Jonas Brothers Talk About Their Best-Selling New Album on Hollywood Records," *SingerUniverse*. www.singeruniverse.com/jonasbrothers123.htm.

48. Quoted in Widran, "Hot Teen Group the Jonas Brothers Talk About Their Best-Selling New Album on Hollywood Records."

49. Quoted in Natalie Finn, "Disney Spells Franchise J.O.N.A.S.," E! Online, September 25, 2007. www.eonline.com/uber blog/b56269_Disney_Spells_Franchise_JONAS.html.

50. Stephen Thomas Erlewine, "Review: Jonas Brothers," All Music Guide. www.allmusic.com/cg/amg.dll?p=amg&sql= 10:hcftxz85ld0e.

51. Quoted in Ed Christman and Taylor Grimes, "CDVU+ Views," *Billboard*, July 28, 2007, p. 6.

52. Quoted in YouTube, "Miley Cyrus & Jonas Brothers—2007 Teen Choice Awards." www.youtube.com/watch?v=kPwj 9yXHQz4.

53. Quoted in Joey Guerra, "Band of Brothers," *Houston Chronicle*, February 5, 2008. www.chron.com/disp/story.mpl/ent/ 5515634.html.

54. Quoted in YouTube, "Jonas Brothers E! True Hollywood Story Young Hollywood Story, Episode HQ [Part 3]." www .youtube.com/watch?v=5IW-5MXQIsM.

Chapter 4: Stepping into the Spotlight

55. Quoted in Live Nation, "Live Nation Signs Jonas Brothers to Long Term Worldwide Touring Deal," press release. January 3, 2008. http://media.corporate-ir.net/media_files/irol/19/194146/ news/Jonas.pdf.

56. Quoted in Live Nation, "Live Nation Signs Jonas Brothers to Long Term Worldwide Touring Deal."

57. Quoted in Guerra, "Band of Brothers."

58. Quoted in Guerra, "Band of Brothers."

59. Joe, Kevin, and Nick Jonas, *Burning Up: On Tour with the Jonas Brothers*. New York: Hyperion, 2008, p. 141.

60. Jonas, *Burning Up*, p. 142.

61. Quoted in YouTube, "Jonas Brothers on *The Ellen DeGeneres Show*: January 21, 2008." www.youtube.com/watch?v=30 Zphu2RcUU.

62. Quoted in *Life Story Magazine: Jonas Love Issue*, "In the Jonas Clan, It's Family First," 2009, p. 10.

63. Quoted in *Life Story Magazine: Jonas Love Issue*, "In the Jonas Clan, It's Family First," p. 9.

64. Quoted in *Life Story Magazine: Jonas Love Issue*, "In the Jonas Clan, It's Family First," p. 10.

65. Quoted in *Life Story Magazine: Jonas Love Issue*, "In the Jonas Clan, It's Family First," p. 11.

66. Quoted in Elysa Gardner, "Jonas Brothers Are Each Other's Best Friends," *USA Today*, March 26, 2008. www.usatoday .com/life/music/news/2008-03-26-jonas-brothers-side_N.htm.

67. Quoted in Gardner, "Jonas Brothers Are Each Other's Best Friends."

68. Quoted in Gay, "The Clean Teen Machine."

69. Reuters, "Jonas Brothers Announce Summer Dates for 'The Burning Up Tour,'" March 19, 2008. www.reuters.com/article/ pressRelease/idUS112038+19-Mar- 2008+PRN20080319.

70. Quoted in Disney Channel Medianet, *Camp Rock*. www.disney channelmedianet.com/web/showpage/showpage .aspx?program_id=3114420&type=jonas.

71. Quoted in Susan Janic, *Jonas Brothers Forever*. Toronto: ECW, 2009, p. 103.

72. Quoted in Ann Donahue, "Six Questions: The Jonas Brothers," *Billboard*, June 13, 2008. www.billboard.com/bbcom/ esearch/article_display.jsp?vnu_content_id=1003816339.

73. Quoted in Ann Donahue and Mark Sutherland, "The Jonas Brothers," *Billboard*, June 21, 2008, pp. 24–27.

74. Jonas, *Burning Up*, p. 88.

75. Quoted in Gardner, "Jonas Brothers Are Each Other's Best Friends."

76. Quoted in Gay, "The Clean Teen Machine."

77. Quoted in Korin Miller, "*Hannah Montana*'s Miley Cyrus Opens Up About Relationship with Nick Jonas," *New York Daily News*, August 7, 2008. www.nydailynews.com/gossip/ 2008/08/07/2008-08-07_hannah_montanas_miley_cyrus_ opens_up_abo.html.

78. Quoted in Vicki Arkoff, "Jonas Brothers: About to Rock," *Girls Life*. www.girlslife.com/post/2008/08/04/JONAS-BROTHERS-About-To-Rock.aspx.

79. Quoted in Sharon Colliar, "Joe Jonas Explains Split from Taylor Swift," *People*, November 14, 2008. www.people .com/people/article/0,,20240432,00.html.

Chapter 5: Living the Dream

80. Quoted in Michelle Tan, "Jonas Brothers Fear Grammy Night," *People*, January 8, 2009. www.peoplestylewatch .com/people/stylewatch/redcarpet/2009/article/0,,2024826 4_20250693,00.html.

81. Quoted in Entertainment Tonight, "Jonas Brothers Interview on Entertainment Tonight," February 10, 2009. www.music istheheartofoursoul.com/2009/02/jonas-brothers-interview-with.html.

82. Quoted in Donahue and Sutherland, "The Jonas Brothers."

83. Quoted in PR Newswire, "Jonas Brothers Announce World Tour," March 11, 2009. http://news.prnewswire.com/Display ReleaseContent.aspx?ACCT=104&STORY=/www/story/03-11-2009/0004986478&EDATE.

84. Quoted in Reuters, "Jonas Brothers Sell a Staggering 800,000 Tickets to North American Leg of Their World Tour," March 30, 2009. www.reuters.com/article/pressRe lease/idUS190250+30-Mar-2009+PRN20090330.

85. Quoted in Gardner, "Jonas Brothers Are Each Other's Best Friends."

86. Quoted in Gay, "The Clean Teen Machine."

87. Quoted in Donahue and Sutherland, "The Jonas Brothers."

88. Quoted in Rebecca Detken, "Jet-Setting with the Jonas

Brothers," March 2, 2009. http://omg.yahoo.com/blogs/crush/jet-setting-with-the-jonas-brothers/140.

89. Kevin, Nick, and Joe Jonas, "Mission," Change for the Children Foundation. www.changeforthechildren.org/mission.php.

90. Quoted in Change for the Children Foundation, "Bayer Diabetes Care Partners with Nick Jonas to Encourage Young People to Proactively Manage Their Diabetes," August 6, 2008. www.changeforthechildren.org/mission_news_bayer.php.

91. Quoted in Daniel Kreps, "Jonas Brothers Unveil Stark and Sunny 'Lines, Vines and Trying Times' Cover," *Rolling Stone*, April 21, 2009. www.rollingstone.com/rockdaily/index.php/2009/04/21/jonas-brothers-unveil-stark-and-sunny-lines-vines-and-trying-times-cover.

92. Quoted in Kreps, "Jonas Brothers Unveil Stark and Sunny 'Lines, Vines and Trying Times' Cover."

93. Quoted in Rob Owen, "JONAS: Musical Brothers to Star in Their Own Disney Sitcom," *Pittsburgh Post Gazette TV Week*, April 26, 2009, p. 1.

94. Quoted in Owen, "JONAS," p. 9.

95. Quoted in Gay, "The Clean Teen Machine."

96. Quoted in Marco R. della Cava, "Jonas Brothers: Good Boys, Happily Grounded, Talkative," *USA Today*, February 20, 2009. www.usatoday.com/life/music/news/2009-02-18-jonas-brothers_N.htm.

97. Quoted in Donahue and Sutherland, "The Jonas Brothers."

98. Jonas, *Burning Up*, p. 8.

1987

Paul Kevin Jonas Jr. is born on November 5.

1989

Joseph Adam Jonas is born on August 15.

1992

Nicholas Jerry Jonas is born on September 16.

1998–2004

Nick's talent is discovered in a beauty salon. He auditions for Broadway shows and lands parts in *A Christmas Carol*, *Beauty and the Beast*, and *Les Misérables*.

2004

Nick releases a solo album of Christian music.

2005

After writing and recording a song together, Kevin, Nick, and Joe sign with Columbia Records. The family is devastated when doctors diagnose Nick with type 1 diabetes.

2006

The Jonas Brothers release their first album, *It's About Time*. Sales are disappointing.

2007

The brothers part ways with Columbia Records but quickly sign with Disney's Hollywood Records. They release their second album, *Jonas Brothers*, which becomes a hit. The brothers perform as the opening act on Miley Cyrus's Best of Both Worlds Tour.

2008

With their popularity soaring, the Jonas Brothers sign a mega touring deal with Live Nation. They headline two major, sold-out tours. Their third album, *A Little Bit Longer*, debuts at number one. The brothers also star in the Disney movie *Camp Rock*.

2009

The Jonas Brothers are nominated for a Best New Artist Grammy. They release a feature film, *Jonas Brothers: The 3D Concert Experience*. Their television show, *JONAS*, premieres on the Disney Channel. The band also releases its fourth album, *Lines, Vines, and Trying Times*, and embarks on a new world tour.

For More Information

Books

Susan Janic, *Jonas Brothers Forever: The Unofficial Story of Kevin, Joe & Nick*. Toronto: ECW, 2009. This biography offers lots of quotes and details about the brothers.

Joe, Kevin, and Nick Jonas, *Burning Up: On Tour with the Jonas Brothers*. New York: Hyperion, 2008. As told by the Jonas Brothers, this book offers a glimpse into the Jonas Brothers' life on tour.

Maggie Marron, *Jonas Brothers*. New York: Scholastic, 2009. This paperback biography has pictures, information, and fast facts about the Jonas Brothers.

Lexi Ryals, *Jammin' with the Jonas Brothers*. New York: Penguin, 2008. This paperback follows the Jonas Brothers' life and career.

Web Sites

Entertainment Weekly (www.ew.com). Features the latest news about the Jonas Brothers and other celebrities.

Jonas Brothers (www.jonasbrothers.com). The is the official band Web site, with the latest news, photos, and comments from the Jonas Brothers.

People (www.people.com). More news and features about the Jonas Brothers and other celebrities.

About the Author

Carla Mooney is the author of several books and articles for young readers. She lives in Pittsburgh, Pennsylvania, with her husband and three children, who are crazy Jonas Brothers fans. You can visit her online at www.carlamooney.com.